BUILDING YOUR DREAM HORSE

BUILDING YOUR DREAM HORSE

*Charles Wilhelm's Ultimate
Foundation Training*

CHARLES WILHELM WITH
ALLISON W. HOUSTON

Howell
Book House™

Copyright © 2005 by Wiley Publishing, Inc., Hoboken, New Jersey. All rights reserved.

Howell Book House
Published by Wiley Publishing, Inc., Hoboken, New Jersey

For general information on our other products and services or to obtain technical support please contact our Customer Care Department within the U.S. at (800) 762-2974, outside the U.S. at (317) 572-3993 or fax (317) 572-4002.

Wiley also publishes its books in a variety of electronic formats. Some content that appears in print may not be available in electronic books. For more information about Wiley products, please visit our web site at www.wiley.com.

Library of Congress Cataloging-in-Publication Data:

Wilhelm, Charles, date.
    Building your dream horse : Charles Wilhelm's Ultimate Foundation Training / Charles Wilhelm and Allison W. Houston.
        p. cm.
    Includes index.
    ISBN 0-7645-7915-0 (paper: alk. paper)
    1. Horses—Training. 2. Horsemanship. I. Houston, Allison W. II. Title.
    SF287.W72 2005
    636.1'0835—dc22

                                                                        2004024049

Cover Design: Wendy Mount

Printed in the United States of America

10 9 8 7 6 5 4 3 2

This book is dedicated first and foremost to my God, who makes everything possible. And then to the many other special people in my life who have made it possible for me to be living my dream of being a horseman. I wish I could name all of you who have made my life so rich and blessed.

To my family and staff, your commitment in helping to run this business is what makes it a success.

To my wife, Anne, whose unwavering support and love keep me going through every high and low—I love you very much, Honey-Bunny.

To my son and daughter-in-law, Jeff and Severine, who put in such long hours with the daily grind type of maintenance that keeps the ranch running—much love and appreciation to you both.

To Karen Werth, my operations manager, you are truly indispensable and I cannot begin to express my gratitude for all that you do and for your endless patience.

To Allison Houston, who has given a written voice to my life's work by co-authoring this book, thanks for being persistent, consistent, and knowledgeable in an area where I am not.

To John and Carleen Enyedy, who have provided ongoing spiritual support, something I need very much to keep everything in its proper perspective.

To the countless clients with whom I have worked over the years, your horses and your stories are what make every day such a complete joy and exciting challenge.

Contents

4

It's Never, Ever the Horse's Fault   127

Appendix: The Charles Wilhelm Training Facility   173
Success through Knowledge

Index   183

Foreword

An Extraordinary Man for Horses and People

I met Charles Wilhelm pretty much the same way he meets most of his clients: a phone call, e-mail, or chance encounter at a horse exposition that starts out something along the lines of this conversation:

"Help, Mr. Wilhelm! I don't know what to do. My horse _____." Into that blank, you can insert any of these all-too-familiar scenarios: bucks, rears, spooks, won't trailer load, is heavy on the bit, needs to be started under saddle, doesn't engage, is buddy sour, crow hops, won't collect, pulls back, refuses jumps, is cinchy, and so on. You could insert just about any issue into that sentence and chances are, someone has talked to Charles about how to fix it—and he has. A recent example was a call for help that came from a nice woman desperate for training assistance because her horse would allow her to mount only after he had been blindfolded. He was "fine" once she was in the saddle, but unless his eyes were completely covered, he would rear and kick when someone tried to climb onto his back. I'm still wondering how she discovered that trick worked in the first place!

But these kinds of calls for help come to Charles all the time, because that is what he does and in some ways, what he *is*. He's a problem-solver. Charles is one of the few horsemen who specialize in reschooling horses with severe problem behaviors. And frankly, that typically means reschooling owners and handlers at the same time. He runs a full-time training operation in California's Bay Area and is often both the last resort and the first hope for discouraged horse owners.

In addition to working intensely with a variety of equestrian issues, his same methodology (collectively known as Ultimate Foundation Training) is also the base program for starting horses under saddle as well as achieving performance improvement for top competitive horses in many disciplines. Whatever the training goal may be, each and every horse goes through his Ultimate Foundation Training program.

My own "Help, Mr. Wilhelm!" call came about three years ago. Eighteen months earlier I had purchased a palomino gelding who was supposed to be perfect for beginners. You will hear a bit more about him later in this book, but the short story is that he had a truly violent bucking problem that three other trainers had not been able to resolve. The last trainer prior to Charles actually recommended that I euthanize him.

Through a fluke of Internet equestrian chat rooms (of all things), a virtual stranger passionately recommended that I talk to Charles Wilhelm before giving up entirely. Though I had not yet heard of Charles, I visited his Web site and decided to e-mail him. We eventually talked on the phone at length, and finally I decided to give it one last try by sending my horse to him for extended training.

In short, the experience was such an amazing success that not only have I sent three other horses (and a mule) to Charles for varying degrees of training, but I have also attended dozens of his clinics and have spent hundreds of hours at the ranch observing his work. I discovered that I didn't just find an exceptional horse trainer, I found an extraordinary *people trainer*. I was so impressed by the work he does with "regular folk" and their horses that we began talking about how he could do more to promote his methods for the many people who can't get to his clinics and demonstrations. He has already begun releasing a wonderful video series, so a book on his training program seemed an obvious next choice.

But as with many of his peers, Charles faced two impediments. First, like most great horsemen, he prefers working with a horse over being stuck in front of a computer. Second, he simply did not have the time. So we decided to put my writing background to use. As Charles worked over the last year, I followed him around with pen in hand, taking dictation from the outside of the round pen, asking questions while he lunged a horse, and copying down running commentary as he taught horses to give and owners to correctly *ask* for that give. This book was very much written by Charles while he was doing the actual work.

The Ultimate Foundation Training program is a comprehensive methodology that Charles has developed over the years. The program is applicable for novice and experts alike, and the methods are universal to *every* equestrian discipline. Whether the horse is a reiner, jumper, dressage schoolmaster, or barrel racer, the results are consistent: a lighter, more responsive, supple, and well-mannered horse. The program works for colt starting and it works for problem solving. But the entire point is that this is a program *you* learn. Learning to train your own horse will dramatically change your human-equine relationship. New levels of confidence and respect emerge. "Horse time" becomes even more enjoyable as you find yourself developing the performance and attitude you have always wanted from your equine partner. And the sense of accomplishment from being able to get those results *on your own* is infinitely rewarding. Charles has helped teach thousands of horse owners how to do the training themselves that results in having the horse of their dreams.

So are you ready to start building your own dream horse?

—Allison W. Houston

Preface

How Charles Wilhelm Became a Horseman

Charles was born in Brookport, Mississippi, in 1945. He was raised by a single mother who moved her two children to California, finally settling in Escondido, when Charles was eleven years old. He began working with horses just a year later. "My first mentor was Clarence Chown, who was at least in his mid-seventies at the time. He didn't teach me much about riding, but I sure did learn a great work ethic from him, and I believe that's what has made all the difference in how successful I have been with horses. He just plain taught me to work hard and never to give up. Clarence had a small ranch where he ran a few cattle. He was still breaking colts at his age when I started helping out on the ranch. I worked

Charles in 1957, the year he began working with horses.

for him after school and during all the summer breaks. And I discovered how hard ranch life really was. After that, I stayed with Clarence's son in Escondido, who had a large ranch, and was shown a lot more about horses."

Next came a stint in the army, an early marriage, and a lot of hard work to support a family. "I stayed in touch with horses, but not on the same level," he said of that period. "I always had horses myself and I was always kind of working with other people's horses, but always just part-time on the side."

And then twelve years ago, at the age of forty-six, following intensive heart surgery, he decided to make a huge life change and to follow his dream to make horses his full-time profession. He was the owner of a very successful automotive business, but his heart had always remained with horses. The life-threatening surgery made him take a hard look at his life and how he wanted to spend the rest of it. Just before his surgery, he had bought what had proven to be quite a challenging young Arabian horse, Tennyson. Charles ended up doing all the training himself after being unable to a find professional he really trusted would do the job right. In interviewing and watching prospective trainers, he discovered that lots of them "talked the talk" but few of them "walked the walk."

After working intensely with Tennyson, he discovered that he was actually very good at starting colts and especially good at diagnosing problems, bringing about truly positive changes. "The trials I had training Tennyson really helped make me the horseman I am today."

He decided to risk it all to make his dream become his life's work. The family sold the automotive business and relocated to the current training facility in Castro Valley, California. It has been a long, hard twelve years filled with many challenges, and, as Charles will tell you, absolutely the best years of his life. He has made the ranch a family business as well, bringing added contentment to the

Charles with Tennyson.

Charles and Anne, with ranch dogs Abbey and Tucker.

endeavor. While he describes his wife, Anne, as "non-horsy," he is quick to point out that she is closely involved in his career and helps take care of all the details. "She gave up a successful interior decorating career to help make my dream a reality." He credits much of his success to the fact that she is supportive, handles much of the business, and accompanies him on the road. Additionally, their son, Jeff, and daughter-in-law, Severine, help run the day-to-day events at the ranch, along with ranch manager Karen Werth, who has been another critical reason for the business' success.

Charles takes in a limited number of horses for full-time training and also has active apprenticeship and horsemanship programs at the ranch. He hosts one of the few apprenticeship programs open to complete novices. He notes that many of his clients are women in their forties and fifties who are either returning to horses as adults or discovering them as adults. Both through private training at his ranch and at clinics and expos throughout the United States and Canada, Charles has worked with thousands of clients who have learned how his foundation training program helps to create the horse of their dreams: supple, responsive, respectful, and yes, loving.

Life as a horseman is never easy, but is exactly how Charles wants to be living.

Charles discusses training goals with a new client.

However, Charles by no means feels that he knows all the answers when it comes to horses. He constantly strives to refine and improve his own methods by working with and observing other master horsemen. He worked with John Lyons in the early nineties and has spent time in the last couple of years cohosting clinics with Richard Shrake. "I wanted to learn more about what Western Pleasure judges look for." He attended clinics over a several-year period with Major Miguel Tavora, formerly chief instructor at the Portuguese Military Academy, where he learned about classical equitation. Major Tavora now gives clinics throughout the United States and resides in Australia. "I needed to know something about that, as well." Charles has also had Olympic medalist Steffen Peters and other well-known dressage trainers conduct clinics at the ranch.

"I try to watch as many clinicians as I can. I see that what we all want is control of the horse and the horse to be responsive. The only difference is in the application. My mission is to try to bridge the gap between the disciplines."

He notes that many of the disciplines share ideas but use a different language. He often uses conventional reining techniques on dressage horses and has discovered that some reining horses benefit from balance learned via dressage principles.

Always looking to continue his education, Charles repeats how fortunate he feels that he has been able to make horse training his business. "I grew up in a traditional training world," says Wilhelm. "And I just really like being a cowboy. Seeing as Roy Rogers was my hero, I feel very lucky to be living my life on these terms."

Acknowledgments

The authors would like to acknowledge the professional efforts of those who helped bring this book together so beautifully. First, the incredible publishing team at Wiley: Roxane Cerda, Christina Stambaugh, and Maggie Bonham. Bravo! What a wonderful collaboration this has been. Your guidance throughout each phase of this project has been superb. And a special thanks as well to Charles Hilton, equine photographer extraordinaire. Where there are truly beautiful photos in this book, he is the man who captured those moments on film for us, not to mention selflessly sharing his lunch with Allison's three-year-old daughter during a long photo shoot.

Introduction
Why Every Horse Lover Should Read This Book

Never be afraid to dream big. Excellent horsemanship *is* within your reach. You don't need to be a "horse whisperer" or possess some natural flair with horses. There is neither magic nor mystery to horsemanship. It comes from knowledge, patience, and consistency—all fueled by your own passion and love for the horse.

My passion is teaching people about horses and horsemanship. No matter what the discipline or skill level, everyone benefits from solid foundation training. *Everyone.*

The purpose of this book is simple. Every horse and every rider need to learn the fundamentals of good training. In my experience, that comes down to foundation training. Foundation training allows you to be able to do what you want with your horse, and this book will guide you through developing that foundation on your own horse. What I call the Ultimate Foundation Training program is a set of training exercises that we perform at my ranch with *every* horse who comes in for training. Whether for colt starting, reschooling, improving competitive performance, or correcting a real problem behavior— every horse I train goes through the same set of exercises at the beginning. Why? Because we cannot afford to have any holes in your horse's foundation training—holes lead to problems with your horse.

Over the years, I have studied with lots of great horsemen. What I have discovered is that the key to an ultra-light, responsive, and well-mannered horse is solid foundation training. "Lightness" is an important goal that we should all aspire to with our horses. It means that cues can be very soft, and contact and pressure can be minimal. The lighter your horse is, the more you can do with him, and the more fun you can have. When properly done, foundation groundwork alone will get you 70 to 80 percent plus carry over into the saddle. So I have taken my own diverse horsemanship education and assembled a philosophy and training program that is applicable to horse and rider of *every* discipline and *every* level. My Ultimate Foundation Training program will not interfere with any other training you may be doing with your horse—it will only enhance your horse's performance and make the horse more light and responsive. This philosophy blends the best elements of natural, classical, and traditional training into an easy-to-follow methodology. Exercises are broken into simple steps that become building blocks for the entire training program. Taking a careful approach with small, incremental steps sets up both rider and horse for success.

But fundamentally, this book is about training *you* to train your horse or horses. I have worked with countless people and their horses and have conducted clinics and demonstrations at events all over the country. After meeting horse owners from every walk of life, I am convinced more and more that *true horsemanship training is about people first.*

There is little sense having a horse professionally trained if the owner or rider is not able to maintain (and even improve) the results. Horses learn by conditioned response and if the cues are not consistently given, even exceptional

Charles offers a variety of horsemanship education programs designed to teach people how to train horses . . .

. . . from the basics of round pen work . . .

. . . to the critical importance of groundwork . . .

. . . through one of many despooking exercises . . .

. . . and even teaches how to have a safe first ride on a
young horse!

professional training will not hold up. Folks wonder all the time why this terrific
horse they bought starts acting up after a few weeks or months. There's no mystery to it—the owners didn't maintain the training cues. It happens all the time
and unfortunately, very good horses fall victim. They go from home to home,
picking up more poor behaviors as a result of poor communication from each
owner.

Guess what? It's never, *ever* the horse's fault. Horsemanship is about *us*
doing it right—you and I knowing how to get the response we want from the
horse. There is no magic to horse training, or if there is, the magic is in you and
it comes simply from being *knowledgeable, patient, and consistent*.

There are four chapters in this book.

Chapter 1, "Understanding the Horse"

Chapter 2, "Understanding Foundation Training"

Chapter 3, "Ultimate Foundation Training"

Chapter 4, "It's Never, Ever the Horse's Fault"

The meat and bones of the book is the training program I outline in chapter 3, "Ultimate Foundation Training." However, before beginning those exercises, it is important that you have a solid grasp of the fundamental principles
that will make those exercises successful.

In chapter 1, "Understanding the Horse," I cover the three primary aspects
of the horse: the emotional, mental, and physical aspects. I am a firm believer

that the emotional aspect is a key factor to many horse behaviors and misbe-haviors. This is where I believe a lot of horse training methods fall short—not enough attention is paid to the horse's emotional state. You must truly under-stand horses before you start training them. Even though my training *philosophy* is the same for every horse, the *application* of each exercise within the program and how I approach the steps may vary greatly depending on the characteris-tics of each horse.

From there I discuss horse personalities. Yes, horses do have personalities. And just like people, some are far more enjoyable than others. But whether your horse will be voted most likely to succeed, class clown, or the local bully, you must understand his disposition to effectively train him.

Next, I discuss the critical role conditioned response plays in horse behav-ior and training. Enough cannot be said about why conditioned response makes it all work (or fail). Conditioned response is the equivalent of building push buttons on your horse. By asking consistently for a desired behavior and rewarding when you get it, you will condition the horse to perform that behav-ior (response) every time he is asked. Last, I will share with you what I believe are the ten secrets that every horse would love his rider/handler to know and use.

In chapter 2, "Understanding Foundation Training," I discuss the key con-cepts of foundation training and why it is so critical for every horse to have a solid foundation. Many ideas may sound familiar; certainly John Lyons, Clinton Anderson, and other prominent horsemen all promote foundation methods. What you will find, though, is that while the language and principles are very similar, the actual applications are different. I present the concepts so that everyone understands the principles and can go home and successfully replicate the exercises with their own horse. I'm far more interested in teach-ing people to train horses than I am in training horses for people.

Then I review the concept of "natural" horsemanship—probably one of the most overused words in the equine profession these days—and what natu-ral horsemanship means in practical terms when talking about foundation training. An overview of my program follows, and I wrap up this section on preparing for the exercises with a discussion on training aids and equipment that I call "No Magic Gadgets: The Role of Equipment in Horse Training."

In chapter 3, "Ultimate Foundation Training," I get down to work and the real fun begins. While sharing some of my real-life experiences with foundation training, I guide you through the actual hands-on exercises that you will use as

Chances are, if you are having fun, so is your horse!

Happiness is a warm, fuzzy yak. Oh wait, that's Allison on her Icelandic.

Horses can make family bonding time even more special.

Karen cantering bridleless demonstrates why "light" equals fun!

Sometimes the best time with your horse is just hanging out and being silly.

building blocks for your own Ultimate Foundation Training program. The ideas and techniques are discussed in conjunction with pictures demonstrating the lesson. Hopefully the combination of the step-by-step directions and visual aids will provide you with a clear understanding and blueprint of each exercise so you can practice with your own horse. The end result (along with your hard work, patience, and consistency) should be that you will have a far greater ability to positively change the behavior, performance, and attitude of your horse, to in fact help turn him into the horse of your dreams!

Chapter 4, "It's Never, Ever the Horse's Fault," explains how to make your dream horse a reality by buying the right horse for yourself, being mentally prepared to work with your horse, solving some common behavioral issues that may emerge, and selecting a trainer you can feel confident working with if all else fails.

Keep in mind these golden rules as you begin working with your horse:

- **Safety first.** Never, ever put yourself or your horse in danger. This rule takes precedence over any of the other rules.

- **Everything you do with your horse, *everything*, is a training opportunity.**

- **End a training session only when you have seen significant improvement.** This is *not* the same as the old adage "end on a good note." Ending on a good note is *not* enough. You need to have higher expectations than that for both yourself and your horse. The time to end a training session is only when you have achieved notable progress.

- **Never go on to the next exercise until you have fully mastered the current one.** There is a reason they occur in a particular order. Foundation training is like creating a building: you must first lay down specific elements that provide the stability, direction, and structural integrity you need.

- **Always make the time with your horse fun.** Chances are that if you are bored, frustrated, or unhappy, your horse is, too.

- **Lastly, dream big when it comes to what you can accomplish with your horse and your life.**

1

Understanding the Horse

THE EMOTIONAL, MENTAL, AND PHYSICAL ASPECTS OF THE HORSE

The emotional, mental, and physical aspects of each horse you come into contact with will be the most important information you have to successfully train that horse. You must evaluate each of these aspects carefully and apply each training exercise based on the horse's unique combination of these characteristics. The more time you take to understand how your horse reacts, thinks, and moves, the more successful you will be with his training and your relationship.

Let's look at each aspect and how it relates to training your horse.

The Emotional Aspect

I want to first talk about a horse's emotional makeup. Emotional control is my favorite topic for two reasons. First, it is one of the most important facets of horsemanship that every rider or handler must understand thoroughly. Second, I believe it is also one of the least understood areas within horsemanship, with very few trainers and clinicians focusing much (if at all) on it.

My career as a horseman grew out of struggles with emotional control issues I was having with my own horse, Tennyson. Tennyson is a very emotionally "high" horse, meaning he is extremely fearful, and only through countless training exercises did I begin to understand the importance of emotional control and the emotional aspect of the horse. My interest in this topic remains strong to this day. The challenges in this area led to my becoming a specialist in reschooling problem horses—something that less than 10 percent of working horse trainers do. Working with problem horses is all about mastering emotional control.

As an emotionally high horse, Tennyson requires consistent maintenance with emotional control exercises. Some days you would never guess he has crossed tarps thousands of times before. Here is a classic example of one of his "Hey, what is that thing?" kind of days.

Through subtle pressure and release cues, I allow him to increase his comfort level of the scary object. My body positioning remains very relaxed so as not to add fuel to his tension.

Always allow horses to sniff an object they are apprehensive about before asking them to cross over it.

Regular emotional control exercises help raise and lower the emotional level under controlled conditions, while reinforcing training cues. This gives you a huge safety edge when something occurs that causes your horse to become fearful.

So, what is emotional control? Emotional control is working with and crafting cues around the horse's own flight mechanism—her natural survival instinct. Horses are prey animals. Evolution has bred them to flee when they get scared. When I talk about horses' emotional level, I am referring to how intensely they react to fear and how fearful they are. Every horse has an emotional level—no exceptions. However, a combination of personality, breeding, maturity, and (maybe) trauma will determine an individual horse's particular emotional level.

I use a scale of one to ten to assess a horse's emotional level. A score of one would be for the most laid-back, nonfearful horse you can imagine; a ten might be for a horse who bolts when a good stiff wind blows. If you have a horse who's good-natured and of good breeding, he can be a two naturally. However, there are plenty of high-strung horses with extremely strong flight mechanisms who seem to score a twelve. I've had more than a few of them come through my training facility.

A low emotional level does not equal a "good" horse nor does a high number equal a "bad" horse. The measurements tell us what we need to do to have a safe and responsive partner. Differing emotional levels usually mean a different *application* of the training principles.

It's critical to address the emotional level of the horse and to achieve emotional control for safety's sake. Understanding and controlling your horse's emotional level will help you achieve maximum performance.

The safety issue should be obvious. You must have every ounce of control available to give you an edge if your horse reacts to fear by bolting, bucking, rearing, crow hopping, etc. Working your horse regularly with emotional control exercises, commonly known as despooking or sacking out, can save your life by having your horse listen and respond when you need her to.

Concerning competitive performance, the issue is very simple. Any horse experiencing fear and anxiety is not supple and not performing at her best. Fear makes horses stiff and tense throughout the entire body, which interferes with performance no matter what discipline you ride.

So, as mentioned previously, the main ingredients that determine the emotional level of the horse are breeding, maturity, possibly trauma, and personality.

Breeding is a tough issue. Plenty of breeders bring horses into this world who may be physically sound but are emotional wrecks. You cannot, of course, change their breeding (other than being a skilled and cautious breeder in advance); you can only work with what the horse has already.

Maturity is typically a matter of age and all the experiences that come with having lived life longer. Just like humans, as horses get older they are more likely to develop a "been there, done that" attitude and to become more complacent and less fearful.

Owning an emotional horse is not a bad thing. Tennyson's high emotional level also promotes his tendency to be extremely light and responsive.

Trauma is another tough situation. Often, people have a horse who experienced a traumatic event that they know nothing about. We can clearly observe that the horse is extremely fearful of specific objects or situations, but we may not know that the horse was abused in the past or was in a bad accident.

But the most interesting factor of a horse's emotional level is her personality type, as you'll see later in this chapter. The emotional level is tied to the horse's responsiveness to training. This is another good reason to understand the horse's emotional aspect. You have probably heard horses referred to as cold-blooded or hot-blooded. "Cold-blooded" is often used to describe breeds such as draft horses, mules, and Icelandic horses (to name just a few). These are animals who usually have lower fear levels. If we look at how evolution has contributed to the emotional development, we can see that draft horses are very large and predators are less likely to attack them. Mules, however, inherit the fight (rather than flight) instinct from their donkey side. The donkey's ability to see all its feet at the same time has made kicking a very effective defense. Standard and mammoth donkeys are frequently used for livestock predator control for very good reason. They can be quite aggressive with predators and have incredible aim and power. Icelandic horses have been living largely without natural predators other than man, being isolated by the harsh geography. Icelandic horses have lower emotional levels because they have not been prey animals.

The only rule: there's always an exception to the rule. Here Charles works with Ruby, an extremely emotional Belgian draft horse. Her owner acquired this 2,200-pound mare as an adult horse and her extreme fearfulness has made it difficult to work with her. Charles is introducing her to water for the first time so that she can be bathed. In this exercise he is only releasing the pressure (the water) when she calms or "gives" for even a second.

A typical example of a cold-blooded breed. This Icelandic horse has just encountered a tarp for the first time. However, within a matter of minutes, the horse is completely complacent about being covered by it.

This is not to say there are not exceptions. Just like we can have a very spooky Clydesdale, we can also have a very complacent Arab. But in general, many breeds have tendencies toward low, medium, or high emotional levels. The higher emotional levels of the Arab and the Thoroughbred also make them frequently sought after for high-energy events. Likewise, the quarter horse is considered a great all-around horse due to a mid-range emotional level that provides a nice balance as a working animal.

So how does the emotional level work in conjunction with how responsive the horse may be to training? Emotionally high horses are usually more responsive and ultimately it can be much easier to get them to be very light. The Icelandic horse shown on the previous page has very low fear levels but has required more training time on giving to pressure than most horses. He has been especially resistant about learning to give to the bit, meaning to be very soft and responsive when anyone picks up the rein to make contact with the bit in his mouth. His lower emotional level makes him more resistant to pressure, which means more work on getting him to be more responsive. We will be talking about why the emotional level determines how you should apply foundation training throughout this book. For now, keep in mind that the emotional level is a characteristic we use to assess the best application of the training exercises and principles.

The Mental Aspect

While I believe that the emotional level is the least emphasized characteristic in many training programs, the mental aspect is very important also. The mental aspect is the horse's capacity for *focus*, that is, her ability to learn the lessons we teach, and her willingness to pay attention. No matter how calm a horse might be, if she is not focused or interested, then the training lesson will not be a success.

We do foundation training exercises to *keep* the horse focused on us. One of the cardinal rules at my training facility is that you never just hop on your horse to ride. People are often amazed that we all spend anywhere from two minutes to thirty minutes doing foundation "groundwork" exercises before every ride. "But why?" they ask. "These seem to be the best-trained horses around!"

Groundwork is not about refreshing the horse on training cues or physically warming the horse up, though those *are* accomplished as side benefits. Instead, it is a mental check-in with the horse before you climb into the saddle and is the most important thing you can do to have a safe and successful ride. Many horses need only a few minutes. These exercises get the horse mentally focused on us and on what we are asking. They allow us to gauge where the horse's emotional level may be for the day (which can be different day to day),

This photo series captures well the benefits of foundation training exercises for working with the emotional and mental aspects of the horse. Charles is working with a horse whom he has just met in a clinic. The horse already had emotional issues and the strange environment is making him even more nervous and mentally distracted. As can be seen, the horse is very stiff and resistant and wants nothing to do with Charles.

Fear and resistance are readily apparent in these first several pictures.

Charles continues to work on simple change of direction and go-forward line work.

The first sign the horse is relaxing and focusing on Charles: he has begun to lick his lips and is looking at Charles when asked to halt.

The horse is now mentally joined up with Charles and has become a willing student.

The horse is now attentive and light on the ground.

Charles moves into the saddle and begins to work on giving to the bit and yielding.

The foundation exercises continue to lower the horse's emotional level and keep him focused on Charles.

Within a short time the horse is bending and giving well . . .

. . . and just continues to soften.

The horse is now yielding as soon as Charles picks up the weight of the rein.

In about an hour, the horse is relaxed, attentive, and responsive under saddle.

and give us the chance to assess if the horse is mentally ready to ride. If not, we can do more groundwork, which gives us 70 to 80 percent carryover into the saddle. This means the physical, mental, and emotional aspects we have been tuning from the ground use very similar cues to what we want to be doing under saddle. The groundwork exercises remind the horse that we are controlling her feet, which controls her space and direction, which means we are the horse's leader. That translates into respect, and we are unlikely to have problems with a horse who respects us.

As with people, there are some horses who are just plain smarter than others. Because one horse learns faster, you may have to do more repetitions with one horse than another, even if both are paying attention to you. It can be frustrating if your horse isn't as bright as you would like and you therefore need to take more time training her. Likewise, having a very smart horse if you're a novice can be disastrous. I know plenty of people who prefer the extra repetitions required for the "dunce-cap" horse over being outsmarted. It can be a humbling experience when you discover that your horse has trained you instead of the other way around, which can happen easily to beginning riders who may not recognize when a horse is working them. A common example of this is at the mounting block. A smart horse learns quickly that she can avoid being ridden by walking away from the mounting block when a rider does not know how to respond appropriately.

But no matter how many repetitions and exercises your horse needs, it all comes down to controlling her direction, movement, and emotional level. Once you successfully capture her mind and control her feet, you have become her herd boss. From that point, you are achieving respect, trust, and even love. Don't kid yourself. Horses will not love you because you brush them and bring them carrots. In the horse world, respect equals love. If you are really seeking a close, loving relationship with your horse, become her leader. That's a partnership the horse understands and thrives on.

The Physical Aspect

What initially draws most people to a particular horse are her physical qualities. These include the horse's natural conformation, coloring, and beauty, as well her physical conditioning. While there are excellent reasons to buy a horse for her physical conformation and overall soundness, many people buy a horse because they like how she looks. I love the old-time cowboy saying "My favorite color horse is gentle."

Countless clients have come to me with horses who were not appropriate for their skill or discipline. They purchased the horse on an emotional decision, making a personal connection with the horse that was largely based on how the horse looked. For example, I have clients who want only paints or black horses; others want only a specific breed. Many people want horses that are a certain height or exact age. The list goes on and on. The biases people have based on physical attributes alone are astounding.

While the horse's physical aspect is critical to a good buying decision, we should decide based on actual need rather than what we *imagine* our ideal horse is.

Any horse can be taught any discipline. However, the conformation—how the horse is put together—makes an *enormous* difference in her ability to

Allison was the first one to admit she fell in love with the looks of her first horse more than anything. "He was one of the most lovely palominos I have ever seen. But if I only knew then what I know now about evaluating the suitability of a horse! Yes, he was and is a truly beautiful animal. But I ended up in the hospital because we were not a good match for each other."

perform. Those differences may distinguish between a great 4H horse and an Olympic champion. For example, the conformation of a cutting horse versus a dressage horse is very different. These disciplines require very different physical attributes. A gymnast's body is different from that of a basketball player, and, likewise, horses with different body types are suited to different activities.

Prior to purchasing a horse, it is important to consider what your goals are and then buy a horse that is physically suited for those goals. Or better yet, physically, mentally, *and* emotionally suited for what you want to do.

As part of discussing a horse's physical qualities, we should also talk about conditioning. The horse must be at the right level of athletic conditioning to maximize performance. The horse must strengthen all the muscles and tendons and be aerobically fit through a comprehensive exercise program. The great thing about foundation training is that many of the exercises, when done correctly, can make significant changes in conformation and help a horse reach her maximum physical potential. I am able to consistently improve a horse's performance as much as 25 to 30 percent through my foundation training exercises, despite limitations in the horse's natural conformation.

For example, a mare whom I have worked with quite a bit, Sierra, is very long-backed. From extensive foundation training, Sierra is now extremely supple and conditioned and can make quick, catty reining and cutting moves just like many short-backed horses.

Different conformations naturally lend themselves better to different disciplines, but foundation training can often help compensate for physical limitations. Sierra executes a few ranch horse moves.

Charles uses foundation exercises to enhance the correctness of movements of this Dressage horse.

In addition to being applicable to any riding discipline, foundation training is useful for any breed of horse. This gaited pony has greatly improved the movement and responsiveness of all five of his natural gaits.

HORSE PERSONALITIES

As humans, we love to connect with animals. We find and strengthen these connections through linking our personalities to theirs. And I can assure you that horses *do* have personalities. These personality types determine the natural pecking order within a herd and they *should* affect how you interact with your horse in becoming her leader. Horses cannot change their personality types. What you see is what you get. Humans, however, do have the ability to adjust how we interact with others. So once you understand the personality your horse has, you are in a good position to adjust (as needed) your personal style with the horse to achieve the relationship you want.

I believe that there are seven primary horse personalities: compliant, indifferent, bully, timid, nervous Nellie, lethargic, and way too smart.

> **Compliant.** This is the horse that most of us want (or should have) and probably makes up less than 5 percent of all horses. This is the horse with the mind and attitude that says, "I don't care, whatever you want to do, just let me know and I'm happy to oblige." The compliant horse gives easily to pressure and has a natural emotional level usually around a two or three. The handler or rider for a compliant horse could be a youngster or a senior citizen. This is a very forgiving animal, easy to train with very low fear levels.

> **Bully.** The bully is extremely pushy. She will have no problem walking into others' space and doesn't care about anything. She has no respect for humans and often little for other horses. This horse requires a very confident handler or rider. Communication must be in black and white when working with the bully horse. And, it is very important to note, if we offer too much pressure on the bully during training, we can actually get a reverse effect: the bully becomes timid and fearful.

> **Indifferent.** This horse is aloof and not social. Once you capture her mind you may well become her best friend, but this usually takes a considerable amount of time and she will never be a true "people horse." With an indifferent horse, the handler or rider must be confident, insightful, and very consistent. It is hard to get the attention and the focus of an indifferent horse. However, once the connection is made, this horse can actually become very nice.

> **Timid.** The timid horse usually seems quiet on the outside, but he will fall apart under pressure. When working with the timid horse, the demeanor of the rider or handler must be very relaxed and quiet. We will need to put pressure on such horses to raise their emotional level, but not so much that

they "blow up." Our objective is to instill confidence in them and to make them feel secure in the arena and on the trail.

Nervous Nellie. This horse differs from the timid horse in that she is just nervous about everything. This horse looks at everything. She has confidence to a degree but is also concerned about everything happening around her. The nervous Nellie is very likely to bolt if you put too much pressure on her, or if you ask her to do things too soon. The demeanor of the handler or rider needs to be relaxed, but you do not skirt around issues with this horse type. An assertive person may need to tone it down a bit (in body language and tone of voice), but you do not want to cater to this behavior. This horse's emotional level must be worked frequently and with greater intensity.

Lethargic. There are actually two categories of lethargic horses. There are those who are cold-blooded with little natural life or energy. You can achieve an increase in energy and forwardness, but it takes work. These are not good horses for the novice, who often does not follow through with the forward cue. If not properly addressed through foundation training, this horse's attitude will become: "If you make me go forward, I will kick or buck." If a good work ethic is not firmly trained into them, they can get nasty.

The other variety of lethargic horse is what I call a "sleeper horse." Beginning riders buy these horses all the time. Super calm and relaxed, the sleeper is fine poking along and appears to be a compliant horse. But what you discover is that in the past, this horse simply never had anything asked of her before. She has never really been required to work and as soon as you start asking her with energy, looking for good forward impulsion, you end up with a real Jekyll and Hyde situation. This horse has found she has a lot of energy and was actually a forward horse, but before she was never asked or motivated to use that energy. The sleeper horse can develop a real attitude. She won't want to work, since she has been trained in the past not to want to work. This can be overcome, but again, while she appeared to be a good beginner's horse, the reality is that a confident trainer with the right timing and feel is needed to get the horse back to its natural forwardness minus the attitude.

Of these two lethargic horses, the first horse is "naturally" not forward; it was not born with a strong "go forward button." This comes back again to a lesser flight instinct and sometimes just lower energy or impulsion—just as with people. The sleeper horse, though, is manmade and is the result of poor training and expectations.

Way too smart. We all want an intelligent horse, but if you are a beginner, you really do not want a truly smart horse. It's not that they cannot perform; the problem is that they find the holes in *your* training rather than you finding the holes in theirs! They are not very forgiving when you are unclear on signals and cues, and they have an uncanny knack for training their people rather than the other way around. For example, they learn quickly that when they do something that scares you, you may back off or cease asking for work. Next thing you know, they are doing that behavior all the time when you are around. It takes a lot of confidence and exceptional timing to make a really smart horse into your dream horse.

Of course, most horses are made up of a combination of elements of these personality types. The important thing is to evaluate and recognize your horse's personality characteristics so that you can most effectively work on her emotional and mental aspects. That is what all of this comes down to: *understanding how your horse acts, so that you know how to apply the training principles*.

The only truly bombproof horse!

Our talk about horse personalities would not be complete without mentioning the B word. That is, *bombproof*.

What is the most requested type of horse? A bombproof horse. Between parents looking for a safe mount for their kids and the huge influx of adults who discover or return to riding later in life (and discover they don't bounce so well as grown-ups), thousands of people each year search far and wide for the legendary bombproof horse.

Clients ask me all the time to find one of these elusive animals. I will tell you the same thing I tell them: there are no truly bombproof horses. There are very complacent horses with naturally low fear levels, and those who have had very solid foundation training added to that natural disposition will be the closest thing to bombproof you will find—especially if they are older horses with solid maturity and life experience to season them further. But every horse in the world has the potential to react negatively to something. And despite the best disposition and training, there is always the chance that the flight instinct will override all else. Riding and handling horses is inherently dangerous. Ultimate Foundation Training will greatly reduce the danger by significantly increasing the horse's respect, confidence, and responsiveness . . . but there is always some risk. Accepting that risk is part of horsemanship should provide you the best motivation for training your horse.

CONDITIONED RESPONSE

No matter what your horse's individual emotional, mental, or physical aspects are like and no matter which personality traits she displays, *conditioned response* is the fundamental tool of the horse trainer.

Conditioned response is the association of a natural behavior (say, a whoa or halt) with an artificial cue (pressure on the lead rope). A *natural behavior* is something that the horse does naturally in response to a cue. For example, a dog rustles through a hedge nearby, startling our horse. The horse shies and moves away. The rustling noise is the cue; the shying is the horse's natural response to that cue—no one had to teach the horse to respond in this way. It's just the nature of a horse. We can think of a cue like the stimulus for the response we want. Over time, the foundation training program establishes a comprehensive set of cues for each of the behaviors we want. Some trainers call these buttons. We have a stop cue, a go-forward cue, a backing cue, a side pass cue, and so on. We will use conditioned response to create the sets of performance behaviors we want to a set of specific cues.

What happens when we halter a horse who isn't halter-broken and put pressure on the lead rope? We will likely get a head toss or an attempt to break away from the pressure. That's the horse's natural response to halter pressure. However, what we want is the horse to stop moving its feet when it feels pressure from the lead rope. So we must train the horse to associate the cue we issue (lead rope pressure) with performing a certain natural behavior (stopping his feet).

How does the horse associate our cue with her behavior? Reward. Reward is the key to this system. When the horse performs the behavior we want, we must tell the horse she made the correct association of cue and behavior by rewarding her. How do we reward the horse? *We discontinue the cue. We leave the horse alone.* From a horse's point of view, the best thing you can do is leave her alone. Releasing the pressure is a very powerful reward for the horse. This is how we say, "Yes, that was right!" to our horses. After a number of repetitions, the horse begins to associate the cue with the behavior that made us leave her alone. When we issue the cue again the horse will perform the behavior that made us stop cueing.

To teach a horse the meaning of a cue, we start with a cue and a behavior she can easily associate. We use the natural behaviors of moving forward and stopping. Let's say we want to teach a horse from the ground to go forward at the sound of a kiss. We kiss while urging the horse to go forward with the wave of a hand or hat, the toss of a lariat towards the horse's rear, or the tap of a whip on her hip. A kiss by itself will not usually motivate a horse to move, but the other actions usually will. When the horse responds with even just one step at first, we reward by stopping the cue. After a number of repetitions of the kiss followed by the reward when she moves forward, the horse begins to associate our physical movement (the cue) with moving forward. As we continue the lesson, the horse will eventually associate just the kiss with moving forward. When the horse can do this 100 percent of the time, without thinking, the horse has developed a conditioned response to the kiss.

Success of the cue-reward system (also referred to as pressure-release) depends on the trainer's accurate timing and consistency in delivering the reward, especially when teaching new cues. The behavior rewarded is the behavior we'll get. We must deliver the reward as soon as the horse attempts the behavior we seek. Letting up on the pressure before the horse moves tells her that whatever she was doing when we stopped the cue was what we wanted. The horse will repeat the wrong behavior when we cue her again. Conversely, if the horse moves and we don't stop the cue, she can't make an association between the cue and the behavior we want. The horse doesn't know that she has done what we wanted. We've missed an opportunity to reward the desired behavior.

Repetitions are important, but there must also be consistency in the training. Whatever your standards are, they must be consistent and you cannot accept anything less. With pressure-and-release training, don't release the pressure until

Karen's goal in this exercise is to create a conditioned response in which she can get Julian, an extremely nervous Nellie, to step on the block 100 percent of the time that she asks for it.

Because Julian is a very fearful horse and looks to Karen for confidence, she works very slowly with him, asking for small steps only.

Once she can get his feet on the block, it's time to release and give him a break to reward him. Then she can ask for the cue again to step on the block.

As Julian begins to understand the lesson and relax, Karen raises the expectations by asking for both front feet to step up and to stand there for a brief moment.

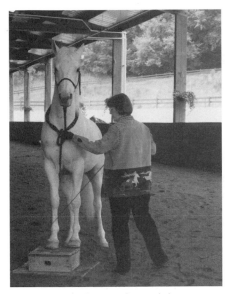

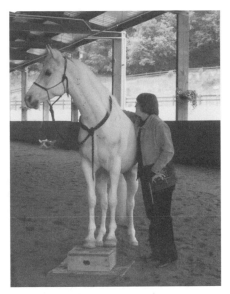

Once again, Julian performed the desired behavior so Karen releases and allows him to step backward off the block (which represents pressure to Julian) to reward him.

By the end of the lesson, Julian is consistently putting both feet on the block and remaining on it in a very relaxed manner.

"Good job, Julian!"

the horse has met your standards every time. It takes hundreds of repetitions for a horse to learn a cue. Counting the repetitions is necessary. There is knowledge in counting. As you start counting, you'll see a pattern in the horse's learning. It also gives you a goal to work toward and helps you concentrate. You can't kinda count. If you have trouble counting, you need to recognize that you will have trouble concentrating on what you're trying to teach your horse.

The horse needs to focus her mind on us for optimum results. In order for the horse to have her mind engaged, we must first have *our* minds engaged. We have to know exactly what we are asking the horse to do—I mean *exactly* what the exercise or response to a cue looks like. If we don't, then we are teaching the horse incorrectly. If there are any doubts or uncertainty, it will show and there will be holes in the training.

We have achieved a conditioned response when our horse gives us the desired behavior in response to our cue every time. The number of repetitions it takes to achieve a conditioned response depends on the horse's personality, your consistency in delivering the cue *and* the reward, and possibly any baggage the horse may be carrying from earlier training. It may be fifty repetitions; it may be a thousand. But the horse is a reflection of us in these exercises, so if we get it, chances are the horse will too. And for the horse to be focused, we must be focused.

TEN SECRETS EVERY HORSE WANTS HIS OWNER TO KNOW

If only I had a nickel for every time I've heard someone say, "I wish my horse could talk to me." These folks are not saying this because they want to have a personal conversation with their horse, but to express their frustration that a training session is not going well. If only their horse could help them understand why the lesson is not working.

For those of us who have worked with horses a long time, we know that in fact they do communicate quite well once you learn their language. Learning their language is easy once you learn these ten secrets, which are really just the basic principles of effective equine/human interaction.

1. **Follow-through**. If you do not follow through every time you ask something of your horse, she will never understand what you are asking.

2. **Control the horse's space**. You control a horse's space by controlling her mind. You control her mind by controlling her feet, which can be done both on the ground and in the saddle.

3. **Be consistent.** You have to ask for a cue the same way every single time. Do not expect the horse to understand and adjust to variations. You have to be consistent 100 percent of the time if you expect the horse to be also.

4. **Have patience.** You can be doing all of the above perfectly, but horses do not wear a watch. Depending on a horse's personality and past experiences, it will take as long as it takes for her to do what you are asking. You cannot allow yourself the luxury of having a short fuse and getting frustrated or even angry.

5. **Be persistent.** If you do not persevere, you will not succeed. If I had to tell people one reason and only one reason why I have been successful as a horse trainer, I would tell them it's because I am tenacious. I simply do not give up and neither must you.

6. **Use pressure judiciously.** You must truly understand the use of pressure—how much to use and what the different forms of pressure can take. For example, pressure can be direct physical contact, like a halter, lead line, or tapping with a crop on the hip; or it can be indirect contact like waving a hand in the air or swinging a rope. Your job is to understand the *least* form of pressure you can apply to your horse that still makes her react.

7. **Release appropriately.** You must understand when to release. Horses learn by when and what we release on. If you ask for a go forward and are consistent, patient, and apply pressure correctly but then you release before she has taken a step, you are guaranteed next time not to get forward movement. Pressure represents anything that is uncomfortable, so all the horse cares about is what it takes to make it stop. So whatever the horse is doing when you release, that is what she learned to do to make the pressure stop.

8. **It's never, ever the horse's fault!** If we use human language to communicate with the horse, then there will be no communication. However, if we invest in learning the horse's language, then we start a relationship and earn the respect and partnership we are seeking. But whatever develops, you are the leader with your horse, so never blame the horse.

9. **Have a great work ethic.** You do not succeed at anything, especially working with horses, without a strong work ethic. All of the above principles require dedication, effort, and tremendous commitment.

10. **Have fun!** Make sure you are having fun as you work with your horse. It's true that in the beginning, it is a lot of work. But as you both progress, it should become very enjoyable as you develop that partnership, and your horse really respects you, wants to be with you, and displays a real willingness to please.

Let me end here by sharing a story with you about a lesson I learned that illustrates some of the principles discussed in this chapter. Some years ago I worked with a gray mare named Zodi. Now, this mare had one of the worst cinchiness problems I have ever seen, even to this day. Have you seen a horse with a cinching problem? Sometimes the horse starts getting agitated with only the saddle on her back. But more often than not, it's just when you reach down to start to tighten that cinch on the belly that she acts out. The horse can feel the cinch pressure and it makes some horses very fearful. Zodi was a classic example. She would rear up and go backward to try to get away from that cinch. She also had a severe bridling issue. When I went to put a bridle on her, she would whale her head back and forth so violently that I had to stay out of the way. She coldcocked my training partner, knocking her flat.

We had been working with Zodi a while and had not seen much progress. I really wanted to give up. I did not see the type of improvement I expected. The owner was persistent, though, and told me the mare was supposed to be nice and asked me to please keep working with her.

Well, just as people have very different learning curves, horses do too. A few weeks later we saw huge improvement. I was ready to call it a success, and then all of a sudden she digressed again. Once more I wanted to call it quits and the owner pleaded for another few weeks.

Well, sure enough, within the next few weeks, we broke through whatever emotional issue Zodi was dealing with concerning cinches and bridles. Not only that, but I saw her two years after she left us. For one of those two years she had been left out in pasture for breeding—a full year without saddling or bridling. Yet even two years after we had ended the training, she barely flinched when cinched up and beyond lowering her head quietly, had no response to bridling.

That lesson really struck home for me and has kept me working with horses whom many other trainers have given up on. Horses *do* have different learning curves and sometimes even just a few weeks can make all the difference in the world. But you have to be consistent, persistent, and patient—and do everything else that makes it clear to the horse what you are asking and why she should trust and respect you.

In the next section, we'll talk about how the principles outlined in this chapter apply to foundation training and developing your dream horse.

2

Understanding Foundation Training

WHAT IS FOUNDATION TRAINING?

What is foundation training exactly? Foundation training is the basis for a horse's performance and behavior—no matter what the discipline is. My favorite analogy when discussing the nature of foundation training is that of the mighty pyramid. In its own way, the pyramid represents structural perfection. A pyramid is sound, stable, and extremely durable. Its composition and perfection are achieved only through careful placement of each stone, building upon the strength of each layer that has been placed before. A pyramid is in fact all foundation, right up to the top stone. In the same way, it is proper foundation training with horses that gives a sound, stable, and durable performance, attitude, and relationship. The discipline is of no importance. It is the foundation that allows you to pursue any discipline on any horse.

As with a pyramid, foundation training works with three sides and the layering of each base. Foundation training requires gaining control of your horse on three different levels: physical (where and how the horse moves), emotional (the horse's fear level, which translates into his flight instinct), and mental (what the horse is thinking). Following the pyramid model, your horse's foundation is the base that builds up as you progress, and the exterior three sides are the three parts of your horse: the emotional, the physical, and the mental. The top of the pyramid is your goal. In between are the building blocks you must place on the foundation to reach your goal. If you take away *any* of the sides or do not lay each level carefully, your pyramid is not stable and can topple. We build this solid base using exercises that teach the horse to bring his emotional level down, focus his mind on what we ask, and perform in an efficient physical manner.

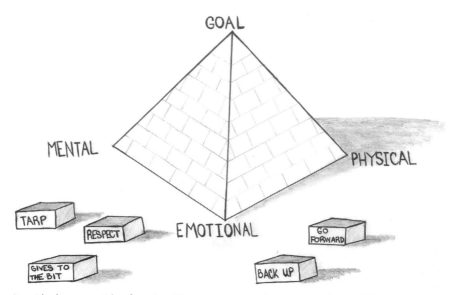

As with the pyramids of ancient Egypt, structure, function, and incredible stability in horse training is created by carefully applying foundation stones in the correct order and ensuring that each "block" is just right before moving on to the next one.

Usually we can manage to gain some physical control of our horse. That is, until something causes his emotional level to rise. The horse's fear can so distract him that we lose the physical control we thought we had. I see people before a ride lunging their horse on a line or in a round pen for up to an hour, thinking the horse won't buck or run away on the trail. But all that physical exercise has not made a significant impact on the horse's emotional level. The horse can still get excited and run away.

Even if the horse's emotional level is not interfering, the horse cannot give his best performance until we control his mind—until we get him thinking about what we are asking. Most horses, including highly trained ones, are not performing to their best ability because their minds are not engaged.

Foundation training is the way to bring down the horse's emotional level and capture his attention to achieve the physical performance we are looking for. Some of these building blocks will be familiar to you (responsiveness, impulsion) and others are often ignored (emotional control, despooking). But with a comprehensive foundation, a horse and a rider can specialize in whatever discipline they choose, achieving maximum performance. You cannot have a complete foundation on your horse unless training occurs for the horse physically, mentally, and emotionally.

In the most practical terms, foundation training is the methodical step-by-step process of teaching your horse to respond consistently to your cues and standards before going on to the next level. Standards here refer to your expectations for his response. When you first start your horse with a new exercise, you will have a much lower standard, or expectation, of his response. But over time, as the horse progresses and understands what you are asking, you raise your standards for what you expect from him, thereby adding more stones to your pyramid and getting closer to attaining your goal.

This is all done through focusing the conditioned response training we talked about in the last chapter on those three primary aspects: the physical, the mental, and the emotional. Conditioned response means repetition—and lots of it. Effectively using their natural aversion to pressure (flight instinct, i.e. the emotional aspect) by releasing it at just the right moment, you reward them over and over until they are 100 percent consistent in their response every time you cue them. Now, I should note that it's important to recognize your own horse's natural emotional level, because it should determine how and when to apply (and release) pressure the most effectively. But whatever the emotional level of your horse, he is ultimately trained by the release of pressure as a reward for the behavior.

So to build our pyramid, we employ the key elements in foundation training: working with pressure, incremental training, setting and raising standards, and repetition. Let's look at each of these elements.

Working with Pressure

You may well ask, what is pressure? What represents pressure may be very different for different horses. A few obvious forms of pressure include a lunge whip, dressage stick, leg kick, spurs, and rein pull. But pressure can also be a person quietly standing a hundred feet away, a car driving by, or even a slight sound. Pressure can be *anything* that the horse finds scary or uncomfortable, which heightens his emotional level and his desire to flee.

So in the most simplistic form, how we train horses is that we release the pressure immediately when they perform the behavior we want. The timing is critical. You must release the pressure within a second after the horse performs the desired behavior—or it's too late.

In this series Lisa is using pressure and release cues as part of a sacking out exercise.

The horse is fearful of the stick with the bag on the end. As Lisa begins to work with the horse, she will only pull the stick and bag away from the horse when he relaxes, even if for just a millisecond.

She keeps the pressure (the bag) on the horse until she gets the desired behavior, lowering of the fear response.

The horse begins to associate the behavior, being relaxed (or at least not backing away), with the release of the pressure.

As long as Lisa does not accidentally release the pressure when the horse is resisting, within a short time the horse should be quite accepting of the object.

The horse is developing a conditioned response.

Consistency, patience, and persistence make the difference in how effectively you develop a true conditioned response.

It's always important to give your horse additional reward and praise for a job well done.

Notice even with the bag right in his face now, the horse has his ears forward and appears fully relaxed.

Incremental Training

In foundation training, we must teach in small, incremental steps. For example, when teaching a horse to go forward at first, we begin by rewarding for a single, tiny step—and we do it for many repetitions. How many? As many as it takes. We never ask a horse to do a more advanced step until he is completely comfortable. Along with progressive steps, we begin exposing them to precues, (a kiss, verbal command, clicker, etc.), so that over time the horse learns the precue and responds to that to avoid the pressure altogether.

Setting and Raising Standards

Setting and raising standards is another important element in foundation training. This goes with the incremental training steps. While you need to consistently reward for the try, you also need to set higher standards and expectations as the training progresses (*progresses* is the key word here). Once the horse is solid taking that first step, move on to having him take two steps before you release the pressure, then three, and so on. Always train with clear standards in your mind, and always set higher standards when your horse has mastered the current lesson. When you have established what the standard should be, you must consistently work to that level and then move on to the next step. Too many people become comfortable with their horse's performance and stop the progression. No matter how good your horse is, try for a better performance. It's good for you and great for him—physically and mentally.

Foundation development takes time and repetition. Likewise, foundation is the baseline to which we return time and again to tune up our horse in the three areas of control. We must do basic maintenance, just like with a car. We make the mistake of thinking that once we have the foundation we can keep building without going back to review the basics. In fact, we need to maintain all exercises taught in the foundation. As with the car, if we don't do maintenance, we will pay the price in performance. At first we have to review foundation exercises frequently. However, the more often we go back to the foundation exercises, the less time it takes to get smooth communication and response. We can gradually reduce the frequency and duration of review. However infrequent the reviews become, we will always need to go back.

WHAT IS NATURAL HORSEMANSHIP AND HOW DOES IT APPLY TO FOUNDATION TRAINING?

Natural horsemanship is the hot equestrian buzzword recently. However, there seem to be different definitions of what natural horsemanship is, depending on who claims to use it and how. But there should be no confusion about the term. It's a pretty simple idea.

Natural horsemanship is *not* a discipline or a riding style. Natural horsemanship can apply to *any* discipline or training program, whether it is dressage, reining, endurance, or hunters. It is not a "Western thing" as many people believe. Natural horsemanship has been around for hundreds of years and it is how some trainers, riders, and handlers work with horses by being *in tune* with the animal. It means communicating with the horse in his own language, not ours. A natural horseman has the ability to perceive the horse as he behaves instinctually, to recognize and understand what motivates him, and to use those natural motivations and common language to achieve a behavior through conditioned response.

Those practicing natural horsemanship are aware that the horse is a herd animal. They understand and use those natural behaviors to train the horse. With all herd animals, there is a pecking order. Horses use pressure and release to motivate other horses to establish their place in the herd. This hierarchy is established in a herd through some type of confrontation. Horses usually move away from pressure if given the chance.

In natural horsemanship, we use another part of herd dynamics, and that is to control the horse's space. We can establish rank and ask the horse to go right, left, back, or forward through control of his space. Natural horsemanship is being able to control the horse through herd dynamics, meaning controlling his space.

Natural horsemanship has nothing to do with specific equipment. These days it is common to use a twelve-foot line and a string halter and that may give the appearance of being a natural horseman, but without the principles they become just another training device. You can be a natural horseman and use a web halter and any length of lead line if you are using the natural horsemanship principles. It is what we do with equipment and how we use timing and feel.

Another principle of natural horsemanship is always giving the horse a way out. There has to be an exit door; otherwise, the horse feels trapped and confined, often resulting in bucking, rearing, or bolting. A horse can go any of six directions: up, down, forward, back, left, or right. As natural horsemanship trainers, our job is to make the way out the direction we *want* the horse to go and to make that directional choice as easy as possible for him. If we stay consistent and release when he finds that open door, he thinks it is his idea. The more we get him to think, the more we can work with the horse.

Natural horsemanship involves simply understanding horses and using that knowledge to motivate them in a language they understand to create a willing partner. It is these basic principles, along with the correct timing and feel and the consistent use of pressure and release that make a natural horseman—not the tools or the appearance.

WHAT IS ULTIMATE FOUNDATION TRAINING?

Ultimate Foundation Training is our collective name for the set of foundation training exercises that we do at the ranch with every single horse. We call it "ultimate" is because it applies to every breed of horse and discipline and because the same program is used for starting colts, reschooling problem horses, and enhancing performance for competitive horses. No matter what the training goal is, every horse goes through these exercises. The exercises blend elements of traditional, classical, and natural horsemanship. We always start the program on the ground, progressing to the saddle only when every building block of the foundation is solid.

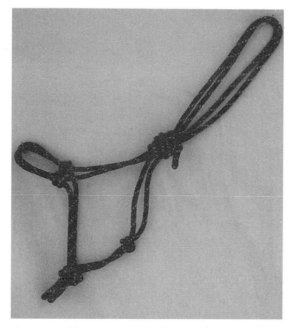

These are all common tools of natural horsemanship, but the correctness is in the application of these aids in the hands of the trainer, *not* in the equipment itself. This is the type of rope halter I frequently use when first starting with a horse in training.

A standard 12-foot lead- line (I use 22 and 30 footers frequently as well).

I recommend using a good-quality snaffle bit 100 percent of the time for every exercise in this book. Again, the magic is in you, in your hands making contact with the bit and releasing at the right times. Going to a bigger bit is never the answer.

First, we will get physical control by asking the horse to move forward to a cue and then move in a circle around us. We need the horse to respond consistently to our cue. If the horse's emotional level goes up, we continue these same basic exercises until the horse turns his attention to us and lowers his emotional level. Once the horse responds consistently, we move on to exercises that ask the horse to move his hips in the direction we ask, disengaging the hindquarters. This gives us the stop. When hip yielding is consistent, we then ask for backing. When backing is consistent, we ask for bending and softening of the jaw and neck while performing these basic tasks. As our exercises become more sophisticated, we start to engage the horse's mind and he becomes an increasingly willing partner.

A proper foundation results in an emotionally sound, supple, and mentally alert horse who thinks about what we ask of him. It also develops the horse physically. With repetition of the circling exercises, the horse begins stepping under himself with the hind legs. This develops his hindquarters, but it also encourages the horse to use his hindquarters to move out (engage). As we progress through the exercises, the horse becomes supple through the jaw, neck, and shoulders. This allows the horse to elevate, which in turn allows the horse to use the hindquarters more. All riding disciplines require this kind of physical movement for optimal performance.

Foundation training also develops the horse mentally and emotionally. As the exercises become more demanding, the horse gives us his full attention. When he is thinking about what we are asking, he can't focus his attention outward on distractions that can raise his emotional level. Only after we have control can he perform to his best ability, and when our horse is performing to his best ability, we can achieve our goals.

As I mentioned earlier, everything you do with your horse is training. Ultimate Foundation Training is about building a complete set of skills on your horse. Everything you do—leading, grooming, bathing, clipping—*everything* is a training opportunity. You have unlimited opportunities to reward good behavior and correct the unwanted. Do not let any of those opportunities pass you by.

What do you want to do with your horse? You need to have a goal if you're planning on doing anything more demanding than watching him graze in a pasture. The goal can be basic, such as just riding on a trail with a safe, responsive horse. The goal can be more complex, too, such as roping, reining, dressage, or endurance. No matter the goal, all horses need the same foundation. Many people do not consider trail riding a demanding goal, yet that activity might actually require a stronger foundation than other disciplines. A trail ride is a trip into the unknown, where we are never sure what lurks out there. Foundation gives us the tools to teach our horses the skills they need to reach our goals. Ultimate Foundation Training then provides a methodology, a blueprint with easy-to-follow steps to make the dream of achieving those goals a reality.

NO MAGIC GADGETS: THE ROLE OF EQUIPMENT IN HORSE TRAINING

Before we get started with actual training exercises, let's take a moment to talk about equipment. If you've had horses for any length of time, chances are you feel like you've spent enough money on training equipment to buy a new horse. Have you ever found yourself lured by trainers at clinics selling the benefits of their magical equipment? Trainer A recommends one type of halter, and it's only $79.95 with a world-famous name embroidered on the side. Trainer B tells you that another style is better. But wait, you also need a dressage whip—no, no, you need a crop. And don't forget about the lunge line; better get a twenty-footer . . . no twelve feet! What are you doing with a snaffle bit? You need a curb bit; wait, more leverage, a port with roller. It's crazy, isn't it?

Before spending any more money on equipment, consider this: These items are just tools. Gadgets, really. The equipment does not train your horse—*you* train your horse. The only thing the equipment does is help you to be more efficient in applying the pressure and release cues that teach your horse conditioned responses. That's it, period. The magic is in you, not in the tools.

So why do so many trainers recommend different types of equipment? Frankly, it's just because they get used to certain things. I use a dressage whip, but I could just as soon be using a stick I picked up off the ground. They accomplish the same thing—if you know what you are doing (although the wood stick may not hold up very well and people would probably look at me kind of funny for using it).

So why do we need tools for horse training? Just like any job, we use tools for building. And what we are building are "push buttons" on our horses. We install a different button for each type of behavior we want. You push the button, you get the response. We have a go-forward button, a stop button, a trot button, canter, back-up, side-pass, piaffe . . . buttons for cutting, driving, jumping, you name it. The key to properly installing those buttons lies in you. Let me give you an example. We can have contractors using the exact same set of tools and plans. One does a lot better job because of better skills and knowledge. Even more to the point, that same contractor could be using inferior tools and still do a better job. The tools help folks, but the magic is in your hands, head, and heart.

Many riders have trail riding as the primary goal for what they want to do with their horses, yet that can be more emotionally, mentally, and physically demanding than many competitive disciplines.

Sometimes trail riding can seem as crowded as driving on a city street. Make sure your horse is as responsive as your car before you head out.

Foundation training allows horses of every breed to become safe and sane trail horses, which gives you a better chance to relax and have fun with your riding buddies.

So what equipment do we need to build those buttons? What should you use? Like other horsemen, I have training equipment that I sell. I may not have my name stitched on it, but it is excellent-quality stuff. However, I don't tell folks that they should buy my equipment. I have it if they need it, but I always recommend they consider the following before buying:

- **What feels comfortable to you?** The hardest thing to do is to juggle all the equipment while training a horse. It feels very awkward at first. I have people at my training ranch all the time, good riders too, who start doing groundwork training with me and get really frustrated trying hold their hands in a certain position, keep a rope at the right tautness, manage a lunge whip with the other hand, and change over hands when there is a change-of-direction exercise. They feel like total klutzes at first. It reminds me of learning to drive a stick-shift car—trying to use the clutch, gas, stick, and wheel all together. Handling the equipment is the same. It takes a lot of practice. And then once you learn it, you can't believe you ever had trouble with it. When you are just getting started, it helps to use equipment that feels the most natural and comfortable to you.

- **What do you already have?** Before you buy new gear, take inventory of what you have. Chances are, you may not need new tools. We all love to buy stuff, but if you have equipment that will meet the need, use it.

- **Do you have good equipment?** I always recommend (which may contradict against buying new stuff), that people own good equipment. While this does not mean expensive, it should mean the tools are of excellent quality. Anything put on your horse should be crafted so that it is comfortable for the horse. You do not want to have equipment that applies pressure on its own! This can seriously degrade your training efforts. The horse will never get the full release as a reward if the equipment is pinching or rubbing or just plain uncomfortable.

So what equipment do you need for horse training? To determine this, you will need to assess your own skills, your horse's emotional level, and his level of training. How does he react to a lunge whip versus a shorter stick? Does a swinging rope get him going or can you just raise your hand in the air and he's moving off? Does he lead quietly under halter or pull away? My golden rule is: *Always use as much pressure as you need to get the results you want and nothing more than that.* You need to select tools that complement the appropriate level of pressure. Keep in mind these rules when choosing tools:

- **Make sure you are safe and the horse is safe.** Never conduct an exercise that puts either of you in danger. Even teaching horses more dangerous things such as despooking, jumping, cutting, etc., can be made safer by working in small steps toward the end goal.

- **Always have very specific goals for each training session.** Don't just go out and start doing exercises without thinking about what you want to accomplish.

- **Be flexible in your goal(s) if you find that your horse is having a "high" day or simply needs to revisit some basics.**

- **Always feel good about going back to the basics.** If your horse is not learning an exercise, chances are your own methods are not quite there. Rather than giving up, step back and revisit some exercises the horse does know.

- **Remember that everything you do with your horse is a training opportunity.** Leading, washing, clipping, tying, grooming—they all give you numerous chances to consistently reward your horse for positive behavior and apply pressure to eliminate unwanted behavior. I cannot tell you how many complaints I get about horses who are perfect under saddle but have terrible ground manners. It's not rocket science why that's happening.

  Everyone is always fired up to get the horse saddled and to hop on. They'll do arena or trail exercises all day under saddle but few people want to take the time to teach their horses to lead or stand quietly. You don't have to make a big deal of it. Just make a conscious effort to do a little groundwork training every time you have your horse out. You will be amazed how quickly you can see results.

- **Ensure that the horse is becoming calmer as the session progresses.** This is a checkpoint that the horse has learned some of what you have been teaching. If a horse is confused, he is *not* calm. When do you know the right time to end? It's time to stop either when you see that the horse is calm and is showing significant progress, or when you are no longer calm and your frustration is impacting the training.

So what equipment do you need for horse training? Since equipment and tools are only an extension, I can assure you that the best equipment is free. To become your horse's best teacher and trainer, you need:

- follow-through

- control of the horse's space

- consistency

- patience

- persistence

- pressure

- release

- acceptance that it's never the horse's fault

- a strong work ethic

- a reminder to always have fun.

Sound familiar? You should find that when used together, these points will work magic in your relationship with your horse. You now have everything you need to start becoming your horse's primary trainer, leader, and partner. Let's get to work!

3

Ultimate Foundation Training

THE ULTIMATE FOUNDATION EXERCISE: THE GO-FORWARD CUE

I always start training with a solid go-forward cue, no matter what the horse's level of training or experience. Why is going forward so important? No matter what discipline, you need to establish a reliable forward cue. Without forwardness, you and your horse are going nowhere. Go forward is the basic cue required for everything you will do with your horse. This is often the solution to common problems like trailer loading, going into stalls, crossing water, or going over obstacles. It's also important to getting your horse to engage (which is getting that powerful rear drive going).

The first couple of exercises, whether using the round pen or doing line work, focus on the forward cue and controlling the horse's feet. When you control her feet, she'll give you her mind. Once that happens, you are controlling her space. The most important building block for foundation training is establishing a consistent go-forward cue.

THE ROUND PEN

The round pen has many important uses in training a horse. It's not just for join-up or hookup. It provides a safe environment for you and your horse. It allows more control of the green or unruly horse, everything from a first ride to sacking out, and the many stages in between. The round pen is a tool just like a dressage whip or spurs, and if overused, it can lose its meaning or efficiency. You must use the round pen to achieve maximum benefits without desensitizing the horse.

The first lesson is to use the round pen to establish directional control of your horse. To demonstrate this I will share my experience working with a

Thoroughbred mare named Harley who had a real problem with her forward movement. Now, unlike some horses, it wasn't that her owner and prevoius trainers couldn't get her to go forward. They couldn't get her to stop! Nothing slowed this horse down, and if she had not been stopped by human intervention, she probably would have run till her heart burst. She had been purchased sight unseen via the Internet and sent directly to a trainer in Oregon. She arrived at the first trainer's ranch with this problem. No matter what he did, he could not get her to slow down. So he started working her in the sand along the coastal surf line. He thought that running Harley in the surf would slow her down.

It didn't slow her down, but it did tear her up legs. And while she may have been neurotic to begin with, the methods used made her far worse. As you know, I like to talk about the emotional level of horses using a range from one to ten. Sometimes I mention a twelve when working with a really high-strung and nervous horse. But Harley was probably my first sixteen. Most horses I work with operate within the natural set of equine instincts and behaviors. Yes, they have a natural flight instinct, but at heart they are lazy animals who like to hang out with the herd and will not run any farther than they have to. Not Harley, though. Something had pushed her beyond that and all she wanted to do was to run away from the world.

On any given day, I could go into the round pen with Harley and have the most relaxed posture in the world. She would still run circles around me like a maniac. She was one of the most emotional horses I have ever met. It was as if her brain was not connecting with her body and she was not even aware that she might be exhausted. Not only did Harley lack a mind–body connection, she also didn't have a connection with any humans.

Working with her was a real learning experience for me. To gain control of that manic body and energy, I designed a specific set of exercises that would gain control of her mind. My initial goal was simple—just to slow her down, even a tiny bit. Once I could do that, then I could take additional steps to establish basic directional control. There have been very few times that I have almost given up on a horse, and Harley was one of them. Perseverance and consistency paid off, but it was a close call.

The approach I used sounds simple. It *is* simple. But with a horse like Harley and many other fearful horses, you must be consistent in executing these exercises. The initial exercise was just outside turns in the round pen. Every two to three laps I would step in front of her to ask for an outside turn. I did this over and over. She would run a couple of laps, and I'd step in front of her to get the outside turn to reverse her direction and then let her do another couple of laps before changing her direction again. The outside turn is the best to begin with since it is the most natural reaction for horses—it's in tune with the flight mechanism and their desire to turn away from the source of the pressure—this is even more true with a very emotional horse like Harley.

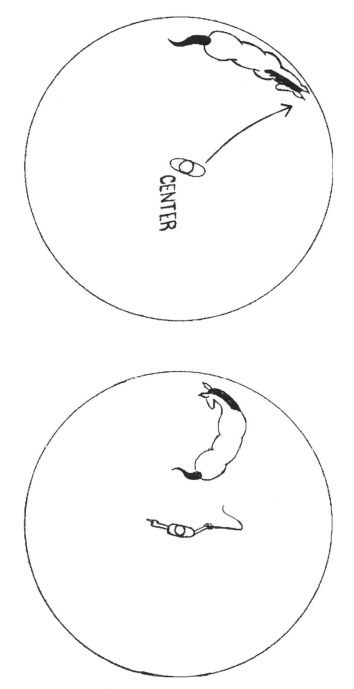

CENTER

This diagram shows the simple progression of asking for an outside turn. What we are doing is using pressure to move the horse naturally away from us, by stepping into the direction it is heading (closing the door), thereby having it want to turn away from us. We can use a lunge whip to enforce pressure in the direction we want the horse to head, and begin to use our hand to point in the direction we want to horse to turn—this becomes a precue.

The following series of photos show Charles in different positions asking for an outside turn.

As the horse is coming around, Charles steps from the center in front of where the horse is heading. You can see the whip pointed forward to provide additional incentive (aka pressure) for the horse to move away from.

This photo shows how to ask a more finished horse for an outside turn. Instead of needing the additional room to "cut the horse off" that we may need with a green horse, Tennyson here is already looking to Charles for direction. Charles need only take one or two small steps in front of Tennyson to cue him to move away from Charles and perform an outside turn.

Then, to complete the outside turn, Charles simply has to raise the whip a few inches to cue Tennyson to continue moving to the outside.

Outside turns are an important first step in getting directional control. However, within a reasonable amount of time you should expect the horse to do inside turns as well. Once the horse is solid on the outside turns, we begin to step *away* from the horse to create an opening that gives the horse enough comfort to move toward you to perform a turn. Once the horse starts to come toward us, we position our body to drive her forward again and back to the rail.

We have two series of photos that show how to ask for an inside turn.

Charles begins to step away to create an open door for Tennyson to come in toward him.

As Tennyson turns into him, Charles keeps his body language soft so that the horse feels comfortable moving toward him.

Charles then steps forward to drive Tennyson forward in the reverse direction, completing the inside turn.

One more time, Charles steps to create an opening for the horse, a comfort zone.

Once the horse is coming in, begin to move to drive him forward.

Continue driving forward until the horse completes the turn and is heading in the correct direction.

Once the horse makes consistent inside turns upon request every two to three laps, alternate with constant and consistent change of direction cues. This gives you exceptional control of forwardness and direction. The horse also starts paying attention and becomes focused on you.

During one training session, I finally saw a breakthrough with Harley. I had done thirty or forty turns before she began to slow. What made her slow was that she was finally paying attention. She was starting to ask, "Now what do you want me to do? When do you want me to turn and will I be turning in or out?" She was starting to understand that when I asked her for a response and she gave me a step in the right direction, I would release the pressure. She was looking to me for guidance; I was becoming the leader. I had finally engaged her mind and her focus was on me. She saw me as someone she respected. My leadership created a relationship between us and with the relationship came a solid connection. Once we had connected, the next thing I knew she was following me around like a puppy dog! Harley was neurotic and extremely fearful. Once she saw me as someone she could trust and respect, she became a very willing student, and more importantly, a focused student.

In sharp contrast to Harley's situation, the round pen can also be very helpful in solidifying the forwardness of animals who are very lazy or resistant to pressure. I recently worked with a Belgian mule yearling named Stetson who is

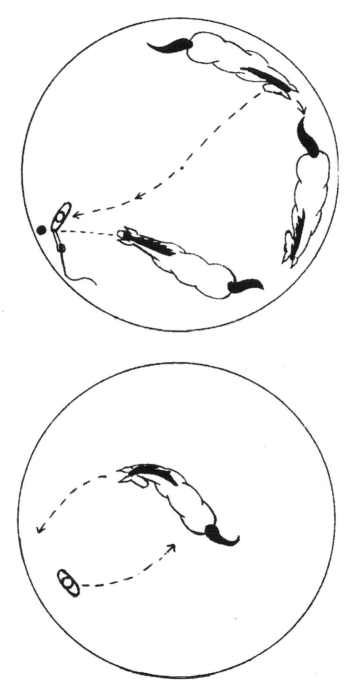

This diagram illustrates the series of steps for both the horse and the handler in executing an inside turn.

a perfect example. Belgian horses are known for being resistant to pressure, and mules are, too, as a result of their donkey heritage. If you breed a donkey and a draft, you can get an extremely cold-blooded mule. These animals can be fantastic for packing and driving since they do not spook easily and these activities typically happen at a slower pace. But for a riding animal, you really want to have strong impulsion and forwardness.

With Stetson, who had a vastly different personality from Harley, the round pen exercises were the same, but the application was very different. With Harley, my body language and posture were extremely low key and calm to soothe her; with Stetson, I needed to be more energized and assertive to get him moving and keep him moving.

In the initial work with Stetson, I used the lunge whip to make solid contact on his hindquarters. There is no point in repeatedly "tapping" pressure-resistant animals—you will only condition them to accept that level of pressure. The trick is to begin with as much pressure as you need to get them going and then to release it at the right time so they "get" the lesson. With a very cold-blooded animal like Stetson, that meant I had to crack him good with the whip a few times. I had to find his response threshold and then reward him for the reaction (moving off). With Harley, I needed her mind to slow her down; with Stetson, I needed his mind to speed him up and keep moving. In both cases, I had them do a few laps and change direction, teaching them inside and outside turns. This uses the physical and emotional aspects to gain control of the mental aspect.

The round pen itself can help these exercises establish a solid relationship with your horse, a relationship in which your horse respects you and looks to you as the leader. The shape and size of a round pen also creates a safer environment for the exercises. The lack of corners and the right amount of space (not too close to get kicked; not so far that you can't move in front of the horse and control direction) makes it easier on both of you.

Here are a few rules when round penning your horse:

- When asking for go-forward movement, ensure that the horse is moving at a solid pace for the gait you are requesting. Do not settle for lazy movement. Expect nice, consistent energy.

- This is never, ever about running horses into the ground or making them so tired that they "give" to you. It is about controlling their minds. I don't care how much you run them down; these are enormous animals and you will never gain control of them mentally by abusing them physically. It is fine to take occasional breaks to briefly let the horse relax during training sessions but make that sure the horse maintains her focus and attention completely on you—even during the breaks.

- Reward for the "try." The fundamental concept of foundation training (as always) is conditioned response to pressure and release. So if you see the horse trying, even just a bit—reward by the immediate release of pressure. It's all about subtle successes and small steps. You can ask for more over time. For example, with Harley the initial progress I saw was very subtle, just an "ever so slight" relaxation and a marginal lowering of the head. There was certainly no relaxed licking and chewing yet, but I recognized progress and rewarded it.

In Harley's case, after several months of consistent foundation training, she became a really nice horse. She was relaxed and ridden on a loose rein, even on the trails.

Another great exercise I always do in the round pen is what I call the post exercise. It's used for a couple of things. It alerts me if a horse has the potential for pullback problems. I also use it to fix pullback issues.

Pullback problems are what happens when a horse is tied up (or even being led) and will pull back away, sometimes so forcefully that the halter or lead line may break, and/or the horse or handler gets injured. Chronic pullback problems result because the horse learned to pull back from feeling confined and somehow got relief when this happened. There are two reasons why a horse has a pullback problem. Either she has not learned to give to pressure while on a lead line, or she has learned to yield but in emotional situations, the fear and flight instinct overrides the training. Perhaps the lead line or halter broke and the horse got away after pulling back. Once this happens, a horse will continue to pull back and look for that relief again.

The trick is to train them to get the relief without giving them the release.

This exercise is useful for working with horses who are nervous around their legs or sides. It keeps us at a truly safe distance, better than a dressage stick, and is good for farrier practice. It teaches the horse to yield to pressure left to right and also to turn on the forehand (meaning turning off the front half of its body, very important in many disciplines).

To begin, I clip a tie ring onto one of the round pen panels. A tie ring is a training tool that allows the rope to drag through it without being tied hard and fast. When horses get excited and pull back, they will feel a drag on the rope, which releases the higher energy. They get relief, but no instant release.

I use a twenty-five foot line. If the horse pulls back twelve feet, I have plenty of rope to go through the ring and still remain at a safe distance. And while I know it's still a common practice, you should never teach horses while they are tied hard and fast to a snubbing post. Horses who are very emotional will injure or kill themselves trying to escape the pressure. My method allows the pullback to get that relief but does *not* release. I have been 100 percent successful with every horse that I have worked using this method.

Thread the line through the training tie and then attach it to the halter. Stand behind your horse, out of harm's way. Next, slowly start to bump the horse along her side with the rope. If she gets nervous, keep bumping until she gets quiet—again, even if for a split second—and then release. You need to watch carefully for that moment to release. Over time, you will increase the pressure, making the bumping and rope contact a little more intense. If or when the horse pulls back, let the rope go and let it slide through your fingers. The tie ring regulates its own drag to maintain some contact with the horse even as she finds relief. Over time, this teaches the horse to tie even with pressure or in fearful situations.

Once the horse is pretty solid on one side, flip the rope over her back like a jump rope to the other side and repeat the steps. As the horse becomes more and more comfortable, you can add more excitement and energy to the rope. Anytime she gets in trouble, simply let go of the rope and let the tie ring do its thing.

You must address a chronic pullback problem if your horse has one. Last year I worked with a horse who reared up when I barely touched the lead line. On occasion, he actually flipped himself backward, driven by an intense emotional state and drive for relief.

But even with an extreme problem like this, within two lessons of about thirty-five to forty minutes each, I could tie that horse anywhere. If done right, this technique really does work that well. In fact, I will initially encourage all the horses that I have in training to pull back on purpose, just so I can teach them this lesson.

If you do not have a round pen, you can do this at a hitching post or any other solid location where you can attach a tie ring. However, you first need to do the line work in the next section *before* doing this exercise.

The round pen is a terrific training tool with many uses. For the early foundation work, though, its most important function is to establish leadership and respect between you and your horse. Once this happens, you can advance your training with your horse. Whether you use foundation training to turn a sixteen horse into a seven or are training a horse for Grand Prix Dressage, these exercises are simple and reliable ways to create the horse you have always wanted.

As I said previously, if you do not have a round pen, that is not a problem. While the round pen is a great tool, it's just that—a tool. The magic to train your horse is not in the tools—*it's in you*. Everything we covered in the round pen can also be done on a line.

LINE WORK

Like the round pen, line work is about controlling space and establishing the respect and leadership required. With a horse who really needs to learn respect, the lead line actually gives you additional control for more effective use of pressure and release. However, while the principles are the same as round penning, the application is different.

While everyone can get fantastic results from line work, it can be harder for the handler to learn than round pen work because you are handling more equipment (usually a lead line and whip of some type). It feels very clumsy at first for everyone. But no matter how awkward it feels, do not give up. Just keep working on the basics until the equipment feels more natural in your hands. This line work exercise is a true cornerstone of foundation training. This training cue is the basis for trailer loading and crossing objects, for example.

I typically begin with a twelve-foot lead line and halter. This gives a fairly safe working distance, while allowing for a high level of control. The shorter the line, the more control you have (back to pressure and release basics). However, with a horse who is extremely emotional, out of control, or just plain aggressive, I will start out with a twenty-two foot line, and then work back to the twelve-foot line as the training progresses.

For example, I worked with a horse named Atlas who was a six-year-old, 1400-pound Percheron-Thoroughbred cross gelding. Although he was a beautiful mover, his ground manners were simply nonexistent. No one had spent any time teaching this horse basic ground manners and respect. He was big, aggressive, and quite dangerous.

When Atlas came to train with me, the round pen was being repaired and I needed to get the results I wanted from line work instead. My initial goals for the line work with Atlas were simple. I wanted him to move forward in the direction I asked, when I asked. I wanted him to stop his feet when asked. I wanted his eyes and his focus on me. I wanted him look to me to give him direction rather than to anticipate. When these were accomplished, I knew I would have gained his respect.

I asked Atlas to move out clockwise around me. Depending on the training and the horse's emotional level, you can use whatever "pressure" is required (a verbal cue, rope, lunge whip, etc.). Use as little pressure as possible but as much as you need to get the horse's feet moving in the direction you ask. No matter what, stay with it and follow through until the feet are moving. The instant they move, release that pressure to reward the horse. Only reapply pressure if the horse stops again before you have asked for a "whoa" or halt.

I had Atlas circle around me several times (anywhere from four to twelve rotations), then I asked for the stop. To teach a horse to stop the feet, you remove the slack from the line and maintain pressure until the horse stops. When you are beginning to teach this (especially to a horse with no manners and no regard for pressure like Atlas), you will have to do more than just take up the slack. You will likely need to start with twenty to thirty or more pounds of pressure to get that horse to stop the feet. Just as when asking the horse to go forward, the key is to use only as much as you need and never more than that. You must also give an immediate release of the pressure as soon as the horse stops (gives). Your goal is to have the horse stop her feet as soon as you simply remove a bit of slack from the line. This takes time and lots of practice. We don't expect success at first. This initial lesson can take up to three or four hours.

Once Atlas had stopped his feet, I paused for a moment. The pause is very important for several reasons. First, it is a reward in itself—a respite from pressure. Horses are lazy animals; no movement is a reward in itself. Second, it helps teach them to look to you for what to do next—not to anticipate. Third, you are training another fundamental building block lesson: the "stand." Your horse must learn to stand well to be mounted, at the wash rack, for the farrier, to be groomed, and for lots of everyday activities. This is where it begins.

After a five-second pause or so, I asked Atlas to do it all over again. Work clockwise and ask the horse to go forward several circles, ask for the stop, pause (praise as needed), and do it all over again. Do not go on to something else or change direction until the horse is moving out and stopping her feet well and keeping her attention on you. Once this happens consistently and the emotional level has lowered, you can change direction and start all over again, but going counterclockwise this time.

For correct change-of-direction line work, which is a gymnastic as well as a mental exercise, you need to pay attention to the nose, shoulders, and hips. Use the following to measure your success:

- **Pay attention to the nose.** The nose should always be in toward you (even if just slightly). This means your horse is paying attention and focused on you. If or when when the nose goes away, pick up lightly on the line, just enough to get the nose back in, and then immediately release the pressure. You may have to keep doing this but do not give up until the nose is in and stays in consistently.

- **Look for balance.** Look for a slight arc through the body as your primary physical goal. For example, you do not want the shoulders either in or out; during line work, the horse must be balanced at all times.

For the proper physical development of your horse, it is important to pay attention to how your horse uses her body while moving. If your horse is balanced, she will neither be pulling on you nor dropping her shoulder inward. Balance typically begins once she is relaxed during the exercises.

- **Look for relaxation.** A key sign that your horse is looking to you for respect and leadership is when your horse performing in a relaxed posture. Common signs that your horse is relaxed include a lowered head, licking, chewing, tail swinging, and a consistent gait that is not frantic.

Once this exercise is well established to the point where your horse truly understands the cues, you will be able to use this as a fundamental tool to calm her down and get her attention any time and place. Whether for trailering, shows, or anything new or spooky, this will become a reliable way to calm your horse and focus her on you.

Once your change of direction exercises are going well, you can make them more interesting and challenging by adding objects. Try adding poles or small logs that are maybe four to six inches off the ground or even eight-foot cavalettis and go through the exercise the same way but incorporate crossing these objects. This is an excellent gymnastic exercise for developing your horse's topline and it starts teaching your horse to cross objects.

In this series we see Severine working with an emotionally high horse on a twelve-foot line. You can see that initially, the horse is racing around her even though her body posture is relaxed and the whip is fully on the ground, so as not to add additional pressure.

She continues to keep the whip low, since this horse needs no additional pressure to go forward.

In asking for the first halt, she needs to make strong contact on the lead line to gain control of his feet and his mind.

Once he has stopped she raises the whip only slightly to ask him to move out in the other direction.

As the exercise progresses (these photos were taken over about a ten-minute period), the horse begins to relax and bend his body. He starts to move with a nice arc, keeping focused on Severine while moving.

He is still forward but is far more relaxed and focused. His movement has lost the frantic pace and he is now engaging much better.

By the end of the exercise session, he comes to a full stop and faces Severine at a stand simply when she takes slack out of the lead line.

Once your horse understands the change of direction exercise, you can then move on to landings. That's what I did with Atlas. Landings teach the stop cue, teach giving to the halter and bit, encourage a horse to be soft and responsive, and promote self-carriage.

Landings ask the horse to move out to the end of the lead line (about ten feet only). You start by having her do a full circle before asking for the stop. Once she has mastered that, you then send her out for just a three-quarter circle before asking for the stop. Again, once that is being done well, you work down to a half circle and finally just a quarter circle. You work the horse on one side repeatedly and you keep at it until she is doing three things: keeping her eyes on you the whole time, stopping when asked, and *not* walking back into you. The goal is to have her stop and stand at the end of the line when asked. If she comes in to you, send her out right away and then immediately pick up the line to ask for the stop. You must make certain she understands the lesson and landings at each stage before moving on to the next.

I should mention that when you first start working with a horse and bonding with her, it is fine to have her walk in to you for praise, affirmation, and a bit of loving. However, please stay focused on the need for the horse to respect and listen to you. So once the bond is established, you must ask for (and expect) your horse to stand away from you and not be jumping into your back pocket. You have to keep raising the standards as you progress with your training.

You may have to practice landings over and over again until the horse really "gets" it. I probably did three hundred repetitions with Atlas before moving on to the next side with him. The tricky thing with landings (this is handler training) is that it is easy to apply too much pressure when you pick up the line to ask for the stop and then accidentally pull the horse into you. It also takes practice to release at the right time. Like all of us, horses start a stop before actually coming to the halt. Reward for the behavior not the mechanics: when the horse starts to stop, that's the time to release.

Landings are also a beautiful foundation exercise for doing figure-eight line work, which is really elegant training work. It teaches your horse to engage, builds the topline, and promotes giving to (lighter and lighter) pressure. We will walk through these shortly. But first, back to Atlas, the horse who had no concept whatsoever of giving to pressure, dangerously invaded space, and was well known for taking his handlers dirt-skiing. Atlas was a second-level dressage horse who had competed well but was such a nightmare to work with that few trainers wanted to deal with him.

Heather demonstrates the mechanics of landings with Sierra. First get the horse moving consistently forward in a circle around you with a nice bend.

Take the slack out of the line to ask for the halt with the horse facing you.

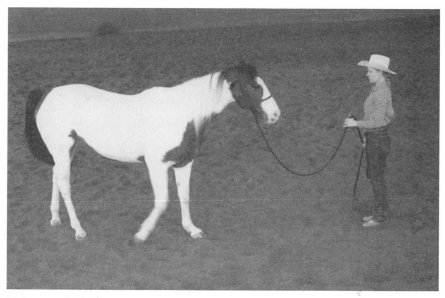

Make sure the horse is positioning herself in a straight line at the distance you want.

Reward the horse for a job well done by giving her a break and making sure you have released all pressure.

After about three hours of line work exercises (with breaks in-between), Atlas was significantly lighter and more responsive. His owner remarked that there was at least a 40 percent improvement in his riding performance. He was much lighter, more attentive, and looking for guidance. He had begun to respect humans and accept us as leaders.

Since line work is a bit complicated, let's review two common problems that can arise:

- **Landings.** If the horse is still pulling rather than coming to a stop when you send her out, continue on that same side until she does not make contact on the rope at all and is giving you her eyes. When both happen, give yourself a big pat on the back because you are doing great.

- **Backing up rather than going forward.** A horse will often back up in confusion. Continue asking her to go forward (with the end of the line, a whip, or whatever you need). Do not release the pressure until she takes a step forward. When she does, immediately release. If she keeps backing and you release while she is still backing, you've taught your horse to back up instead of go forward. Be sure you are standing behind the withers but in front of the hip when asking to go forward. Standing behind the withers drives the horse forward (in general), but standing too close to the hip puts you in a dangerous position.

Once you feel confident about this basic line work and feel comfortable handling the equipment, you can graduate to figure eights.

For training figure eights, start your horse moving in a full circle around you or until the horse is going forward consistently. Instead of changing direction, take two to three steps backward and ask the horse to come in toward you. *Now change direction* so the horse comes in through the center.

If you are using a twelve-foot line, this results in a twenty-four-foot circle. Ask the horse to come through the circle and change direction to the new circle. When you are able to do this without resistance and get the horse to do a new, completely full circle, move on to a three-quarter circle and then a half circle. At this point, you have accomplished the figure eight. Your goal will be to do this on a thirty-foot line.

As you practice, expect that your horse may either stop or slow down when you ask for movement toward you and ask to change direction. First get the horse to understand what you are asking. Once you have the directional control established, you can then ask for the energy and consistent forwardness throughout the entire figure eight.

Charles gets Tennyson moving around him nicely.

Charles positions himself to begin to ask Tennyson to move inside toward him.

Charles removes the slack from the line to cue Tennyson for the change of direction.

As Tennyson comes in, Charles switches the equipment in his hands so the lead line is positioned for the new direction and the lunge is on the other side, representing pressure in the direction Charles wants Tennyson to move away from.

There is one problem that I see with most people when they begin doing line work. This problem prevents them from achieving their desired results. People will let the horse move them around and pull at them. Think of your-self as a wagon wheel or a hub. The horse needs to be moving around you; you should not be moving with the horse. The horse will never learn to give if this happens. Initially the horse will be pulling on you when you begin to teach her line work and how to yield. As long as you do not give and you always main-tain the contact until the release, she will eventually become very light on the line and always move around you fluidly.

Like the round pen, line work is a method to establish your role as your horse's leader. Why is it so important that your horse respects you? Because as I have said several times, respect equals love in the horse world! We have to understand the horses' world and how to communicate in their language. Learning to do this is the responsibility of every horseperson. Once you are flu-ent in equine communications, you can enjoy the training process and discover how truly fun horses are. The lasting relationship you build will bring all the love you have ever wanted.

LEADING MANNERS AND RESPECTING SPACE

You earn respect by controlling your horse's space, movement, and direction. The next step in enhancing this relationship is teaching your horse good ground manners. This means that your equine partner must respect your space and keep a proper distance when being led, while standing, being tied, etc. During leading the horse must learn what I call the "equine heel." When you stop, she stops. When you turn right or left, she moves with you automatically. When you back up, your horse backs up. It also means she is the correct dis-tance beside you while leading, not too close, and not lagging too far behind.

Everything we did in the round pen and with the lead line work sets the foundation for teaching your horse good manners by gaining her attention. We've now created a willing student. But why are ground manners so impor-tant? I've already told you about Atlas, a horse who was aggressive toward peo-ple. With him, the need for respect and manners was obvious. But I'm going to introduce you to Patch, one of the sweetest, most people-loving horses you could ever know. It should become equally clear why a horse like this needs solid ground manners.

Patch was actually my horse. I got him as yearling; he's about three now. He's a solid and stocky Paint gelding with blue eyes and just a few black patches on an otherwise white coat. He'd been raised by his prior owners from the time he was a weanling and he had been a very special family pet.

Well, Patch adores people; he just cannot get enough human attention. Sounds great, right? The problem is he had been handled so much (petted, cuddled, kissed, you name it) that when I got him, he had no concept of pressure or respect, and his favorite place to be was in your back pocket. The closer he could get to you the better, no matter if he was stepping on you or knocking you down. He'd do anything for more attention and loving. There is not a mean bone in this horse's body, but he demanded constant handling and would be right in your face to get it. This was adorable when he was a cute little baby foal. It's not so cute when a thousand pounds is head butting you for more petting.

Patch had become what I call "dull," meaning he had become virtually desensitized to pressure. He had been physically touched so much without being asked to do anything in return that he was not motivated by pressure. When I initially started working with him, even just the basic go-forward cue required an enormous amount of pressure. He simply had no idea what I was asking for and, perhaps more to the point, had no concept of being "asked." He was not pressured by a rope, lunge whip, or anything else. You do not want your horse to fear you, but she must understand the basics of pressure and release for effective training. As I have said, pressure is working within a horse's own natural instincts, using the horse's flight mechanism to get away from something. But Patch had lost this instinct. So when I first began working with him, I had to use a lot of pressure to reintroduce the simple mechanics of pressure and release. Same as with Stetson the mule but for a different reason.

I started working Patch in the round pen and on a lead line to begin to establish our relationship with me as the leader. The biggest challenge came when I tried to teach him basic ground manners and leading etiquette. Again, he just wanted to be in my back pocket all the time. What I did, and what you have to do with any horse who does not meet your expectations for good ground manners, follows.

Every time you take your horse out of the stall or pasture is a training opportunity in ground manners. Make every walk you take with your horse count. Determine the distance you want the horse to walk beside you. (I like a horse about eighteen to twenty-four inches from my shoulder.) Cue your horse to go forward from the stand with a kiss or a cluck. Do *not* pull on the lead rope. Always give her a chance to move forward just from the precue. If she does not move, continue cueing and then apply light pressure to the line that matches the pressure she is offering (no more and no less). Once she starts forward, immediately release the pressure and continue walking with a slack line. Always walk your horse with a slack line. If your horse starts to walk ahead of you, stop and ask her to back up several steps. Horses do not like to back up and this is an appropriate negative reinforcement. Horses need a reason to change a behavior; backing is a reason they can understand.

Jennifer demonstrates good positioning for leading a horse. The horse's head is generally parallel to your own and about eighteen to twenty-four inches lateral to you.

If the horse starts to wander from the right position, Jennifer simply picks up the line to *maintain* contact until the horse gives; she will not pull on the lead.

Note slack in line.

It's just as important to know what NOT to do! Allison demonstrates some of the common mistakes people make when leading. Pulling on the lead line to get the horse to go forward.

Wrapping the lead line around your hand or arm. If the horse were to bolt, what do you think would happen?

Letting the horse walk ahead of you.

A horse that leads well and safely on the ground is a pleasure for everyone to spend time with!

Heather asks Sierra to show us how to ask for and get good backing, the most useful technique I know for teaching horses not to walk ahead of us on a lead line. Note the position of Heather's hands and the lead line itself in these photos.

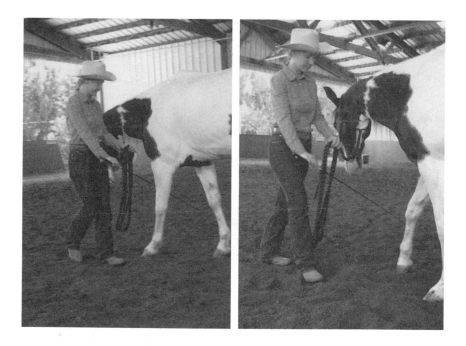

It is wonderful to "love on" your horse—just make sure you are doing it on your terms, not the horse's!

On the topic of giving horses a reason to change their behavior, let's talk a bit more about motivation. Motivation is integral for your training. Everyone needs a reason to change their behavior and that reason, whatever it is, is their motivation. Motivation can be positive or negative, but it is something that compels us to behave in a new way. Relief from pressure is what motivates horses. When teaching them to lead, not letting go of the lead line (and I mean maintaining the contact, not pulling on them) until they give, is a reason for the horse to change. As long as you are consistent in how you ask for the behavior and how you reward when it occurs, your horse will make the change you are seeking.

Since Patch really liked to walk into our personal space, we backed him and backed him and backed him some more. He was always stepping into us when being led or groomed. So we *consistently* responded with back commands every single time he did it. Yes, we did hundreds and hundreds of repetitions and always right away, so he understood why we asked him to do something he did not like doing. He had to learn to stand away from us. Once he learned the lesson, we were able to work on more advanced ground manners exercises such as moving his hips over, moving his shoulder over, and side passes—all fantastic ground manners exercises that carry over into saddle work.

I am sure that because Patch was also learning the basic concept of pressure and release, it took longer than it would normally. But when he did get it, I can't tell you how quickly everything else fell into place. He always wanted to please and get attention; we just had to show him a new way to do it. And once he learned this, he became so light and responsive at such a young age that he amazed us. He has a wonderful mind and temperament; he just had bad manners because of how he had been raised. Now a child can safely lead this horse. That's what this is all about: safety. It's not just the aggressive horses we need to instill with good manners. Any horse who does not respect our space, no matter how sweet, is dangerous.

A client once asked me how much a horse, especially a baby, should be handled. She wanted to know if you could handle a horse too much. My response was, "The question isn't how *much* you should handle your horse, but *how* you should handle your horse." In some cases, just fifteen minutes of proper foundation training can offer a hundred times more benefit than hours of improper handling. While these basic foundation training exercises are applicable to working with babies as much as mature horses, babies like to play. And they like to play a lot. This does not mean they are being bad or that you are doing a bad job training them; it simply means you need to be prepared to be exceptionally patient and understanding.

Lastly, I am not saying you should restrict the time you spend "lovingon" your horse. Far from it! Horses adore physical contact and petting and it's a very special element of why we enjoy spending time with them. What I *am* saying is that the handling needs to be on your terms, not theirs, and in their space, not yours. Can you scratch their withers or rub their heads too much? No. Can you kiss your horse too much? Only if you're a cowboy and get caught in the act; otherwise, no. As long as you control their space and have established the respect and the leadership role, love away on them. Make the most of your time with your horse and continue to teach her that respect equals love.

EMOTIONAL CONTROL AND DESPOOKING

As I mentioned earlier, most horse trainers place too little emphasis on emotional control. It is the key to unlocking so many mysteries of the horse and it should play a prominent role in horse training. A gelding I worked with named Bandwidth is a great example of how recognizing and working with the horse's emotional level and personality can enact positive changes.

Bandwidth is a Palomino Quarter horse who was about six when he came in for training. He was 15.2 hands and very well put together. When Richard Shrake did a clinic at my ranch, he used Bandwidth to demonstrate some areas of correct conformation. Bandwidth had been sold to his owner, Allison, over a year earlier and had been advertised as a true beginner's horse. Like many of my clients, Allison was returning to horses as an older adult and had been looking for the classic bombproof horse. Allison thinks now that Bandwidth had probably been drugged for the sale process because he was so different emotionally after she bought him. When he came to me he was definitely a twelve on the emotional scale. What seemed misleading was that he appeared to be compliant. On the ground, he was very gentle and quiet. On casual observation, you would wonder why in the world this horse was in training with me. He seemed relaxed and complacent. He led, tied, clipped, loaded, and was great for the farrier. However, the minute you added pressure, he fell apart completely. When Bandwidth fell apart, he bucked. Not just a few bucks, either—prolonged rodeo-style, violent bucking.

Allison had already hired other trainers to work with him without success before she came to me. After listening to descriptions of the training methods they had used to "fix" the bucking, I discovered that all they had done was put more and more pressure on this horse without giving him any release. In all likelihood, they actually made him worse than when she first got him. My guess is that he started out life as a nice compliant horse, but because of too much pressure along the way or some trauma, he became a true nervous Nellie.

In Bandwidth's case, even though he was already broke to ride (or at least to launch), we spent the first three months working primarily on his emotional

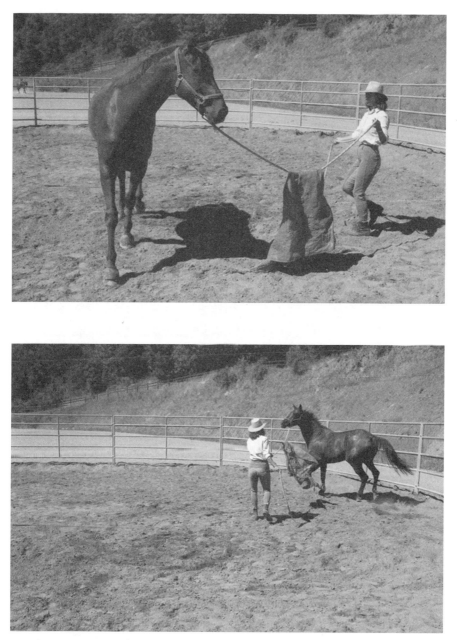

Lisa demonstrates a great emotional control exercise done on line with a tarp. Though pictured here in a round pen, the round pen is not required. The horse is learning to give Lisa mental attention and physical control while having her emotional level raised high. You can see that the horse goes from being nervous about the tarp flapping while she moves to being quite complacent over time. How long it will take for the horse to relax depends on the emotional level and the personality of the horse.

Lisa has done her job well and by the end of the exercise, the horse is pretty oblivious to the tarp flapping on the lead line.

level and we did only groundwork. We conducted despooking exercises to establish better emotional control. Despooking is a more comprehensive method of what used to be called "sacking out," An old cowboy expression, sacking out originates from the common practice of using old sacks to rub all over a horse, cover his eyes, etc., one of the many tools cowboys used for "breaking" horses. I use the term in a similar fashion, but in my vocabulary it encompasses a comprehensive program of desensitizing (despooking) horses to a variety of objects and situations to prepare them for almost anything. In sacking out, you deliberately raise and lower their emotional response to fear in a controlled environment.

We taught Bandwidth to go over scary objects and tarps and sacked him out, stroking him with whips and plastic bags. All of this was accomplished very slowly and carefully. You have to create the conditions to raise the horse's emotional level so she can learn to accept it. But you cannot do it all at once, and if you add too much pressure without giving the horse an out or a release, you have made your own job harder. Especially with a horse like this who seems so compliant, you can be tempted to rush through these exercises, but it's a huge mistake. With a higher emotional level horse, you will have to work longer on all of the emotional control exercises.

It was six months until I knew we were on the road to success with Bandwith—six months filled with two steps forward, one step back. This is common for a horse with a high emotional level. Because of my experience, I did not give up on him as others had done. Bandwidth learned to accept pressure without reacting negatively. We replaced his negative reaction with a positive one. Did it take time? Yes. Was it worth it? Allison says yes. Not only did the bucking cease, but he ended up beautifully light and ultraresponsive. Does he need maintenance work? Yes, all horses do and emotionally high horses need it more than others. We can take a horse who is a twelve like Bandwidth and with regular work keep that horse between a level four and six—a huge difference in both safety and performance.

Another example is a horse I trained named Georgia, a very "timid" OTTB (Off-the-Track Thoroughbred). Georgia was eight years old, a big-boned sorrel over seventeen hands. Much like Bandwidth, Georgia appeared to be quite relaxed on the outside. However, the moment you added certain types of pressure, especially around her face, she overreacted. I began working with her because of her serious pullback problem, but that was one symptom of the same root issue. Georgia wanted to escape pressure and to do so she would explode, whether pulling back, bolting, or simply running away with you. She was very expressive and unpredictable in her timidity and thus very dangerous. While Georgia would not intentionally hurt someone, becaue of her reactions she was not a horse that I wanted to ride.

I started Georgia with the round pen and line work exercises that we reviewed earlier. Those exercises probably brought her emotional level down from a twelve to an eight, but the real work with building emotional control started with sacking out. Georgia needed to learn to accept pressure, especially around her face, and to yield to it.

I begin the sacking out process with objects. With Georgia, I started with a lunge whip, which allows me safe distance. Remember, safety first, especially with an emotional horse. I began lightly touching her with the end of the lunge whip. When she pulled away, I stayed with her until she stopped moving her feet and then I released the pressure. I allowed her time to smell the whip and see it. I spent the time touching her, releasing, touching, then releasing; always allowing her to relax in between. As she became accustomed to the contact, I started increasing the time I applied pressure and made sure I was touching her all over with it.

I introduced plastic bags in the next exercise. She did have a major issue with those. I started out far away with the bags and slowly came closer, moving away each time as she began to back up. After about thirty minutes, I was able to stroke her all over with the bag itself. We have pictures of Lisa performing this exercise in chapter 2, "Understanding Foundation."

The next step was going over objects. A pole or tarp works great for this. I put her on a line and asked her to go forward. (*Note: The go-forward cue has to be solid before you start any of these exercises.*) Position the length of the line and

Note the body language; the horse is
very nervous about the tarp!

Change direction initially at the farthest
point from the object.

Keep at it until horse crosses the tarp.

End the exercise when the horse is
relaxed such that her head is lowered,
she bends around you, and her focus
is fully back on you.

For the next exercise, raise your expectations and go to the next level!

the object so that the horse must cross it in order to move out. Keep in mind that
if she is very fearful of the object, you should start with moving her around near
the object before asking her to cross over it. If a horse is fearful of a tarp or pole,
lay one on the ground where you are doing standard change-of-direction line
work and slowly move closer and closer to the object until you can see that she

is beginning to relax around it. Then, when she is ready, you can move the horse so that when you ask for the go-forward cue, she will have to cross the object. Whether she bolts, jumps, trots, or walks over it does not matter at first, as long as your horse does cross it.

Add crossing over the object to your change-of-direction line work. The goal is to have the horse calmly standing on the object at the end of the lesson. Once you are ready, have the horse cross over the object and then ask for the stop when she is at the farthest point away from the object (opposite side of the circle). Let her relax for a moment and then reverse direction and do the same thing—that is, a full circle over the object. Stop at the farthest point, relax, change direction, and move out again.

As you do this, watch your horse's body language. As she begins to relax, stop her closer and closer to the object until her comfort level is such that she will stop and stand on the tarp or over part of pole. You may go from a full circle, to seven-eighths of circle, then three-quarters, then one-half, and so on. What are the signs that she is relaxing and you can begin stopping her closer to the object? Ears forward, licking and chewing, and head dropping—you should see her overall energy level coming down. Instead of jumping or bolting over the object, she may slow to a trot or even a walk.

With timid and nervous horses, you have to invest the time to build their confidence by introducing pressure in very small increments and always allowing them to relax after each application of pressure. You do not want a horse you have to tiptoe around—they are dangerous and not fun. It is critical that you learn to control the emotional response of timid and nervous horses. Exercise caution and don't put too much pressure on them. Make certain that you always give them an "out" (an escape door, if you will) from the pressure you are applying. Anytime you force a horse to accept pressure without giving them an out, you risk creating a major training wreck. You could lose most if not all of the progress you have made with their emotional level and have a far harder time going forward.

We saw huge improvements with Georgia, but it was just the beginning. Emotional horses are more work. You often need to introduce the lessons in smaller steps and take longer to do it. That does not mean an emotional horse cannot be your dream horse, but you must be willing, patient, and interested in spending the extra time addressing their emotional level. Not only will you need to do that initial work, but you'll also need to do regular emotional control exercises with the horse as long as you own her. Horses don't get "fixed" from these training exercises; rather, they become desensitized to the fear response. Unless you continue the work, the sensitivity returns and a horse who used to be able to be completely covered by a tarp three months ago may bolt after seeing one fifty feet away.

Most horses have a higher emotional level than most riders want. There are more horses with an emotional level in the seven-to-ten range than there are in the two-to-four range. Fear is a natural instinct in horses and it tells their brains to flee. You must continuously condition your horse to have the control you want when you need it. Emotional control exercises provide an edge in that conditioning.

When it comes to the importance of working with emotional control to create the relationship, attitude, and performance you want from your equine buddy, I do know what I'm talking about. My extremely emotional and very high maintenance horse Tennyson was the horse who made me the trainer I am today. I have learned more from working with him than from most other horses combined. People see us at expos and clinics and are amazed at everything I can do with him—and often without any tack at all. He appears so light and responsive and ultrarelaxed. Let me assure you, I have to work him constantly to keep him that way. Sacking out is a key component of our regular training routine. It has to be. There are plenty of days when he acts like he has never seen a tarp before and wants to jump into my lap for protection. But after a few minutes of sacking out, his emotional level is back down to a four or five and his mind is focused back on me and what I am asking him to do. When that happens, I have a safe and fun horse. I love Tennyson and would not trade him for anything. He is definitely more work than most horses would be, but he has taught me more than most trainers have learned. I figure that's a pretty good deal for both of us.

Work on despooking and crossing objects can also just be fun!

GIVING TO THE BIT

The foundation exercises we have covered so far are all necessary to set your horse up for success, whether for her first ride or for reschooling. The exercises brought down your horse's emotional level, established solid groundwork and respect, and lowered the horse's resistance. Now the horse is far more ready and willing when we are ready to ride. Remember that before you begin to work your horse with a snaffle bit, your horse must have a solid go-forward cue and you must also be able to stop her feet on the line. With these fundamentals, we have control and the horse has already begun to yield to us. While everyone has strong opinions about bits, for every exercise that requires a bit, I use and recommend a snaffle all the time. I do not believe in using stronger bits to solve problems.

One important factor is your hand position. Hand position can make all the difference. Proper hand position really can give you control of the horse. Having the correct hand position allows you to tell the horse when she has the right idea and that she is doing what you want her to do. When your hands are out of position, you can't send the proper signals to the horse at the time the signal needs to be sent. Work on keeping your hands in the safest position *and* in the position that is best for teaching the horse. The natural place to put your hands is not where your hands are supposed to be. Your hands communicate with the horse. They belong no higher than six inches above the saddle horn, no farther forward than six inches in front or behind the saddle horn, and no farther to either side than six inches from the saddle horn. (It's like working with your hands inside a six-inch box. The radius is six inches with the saddle horn at the center of the sphere). You can go outside the box to make corrections, but then your hands must go back in when done.

The clearer your knowledge and understanding are, the clearer you will be with your signals. You have to know the lesson in order to teach it. You have to know the components of giving to know if the horse is doing what you are asking. Develop a lesson plan for teaching your horse to give to the bit that follows this overall progression. The sequence is

1. Teach the horse to give to the bit at a standstill

2. Teach the horse to walk and give to the bit.

3. Teach the horse to walk and give to the bit longer.

4. Teach the horse to trot and give to the bit.

5. Teach the horse to canter and give to the bit.

Teach the horse one thing at a time. Walking and giving to the bit are two things; standing still and giving to the bit are two things. Giving to the bit is one thing. When you begin teaching the horse to give to the bit, it doesn't matter what her feet do. Concentrate only on giving to the bit. This method is called "singleness of purpose," which means deciding on a specific lesson to teach and not varying from the plan. Do not stray from the single goal or purpose you are trying to teach your horse.

The order of performance works like this

1. Your concentration comes first.

2. Your consistency comes next.

3. Next comes the horse's consistency.

4. Finally comes the horse's concentration.

You have to decide what you are teaching the horse and concentrate on that lesson alone. Don't become upset with the horse for being distracted by something when you are also looking at her distraction.

In practical terms, giving to the bit is made up of three different components: R-R-C: Recognition, Response, and Control.

- **Recognition.** The horse recognizes the signal and thinks the signal is important.

- **Response.** The horse gives a specific response, and the body part comes alive and moves where you want.

- **Control.** The horse turns over control of the specific part of her body.

The next thing you will teach the horse is the "baby-give." The components of the baby-give are

- No pull from the horse.

- Movement or energy in the body part and that body part moving in the direction you want it to move (i.e., the jawbone comes alive and moves directly underneath the bit, on the opposite side of the rein you are picking up on).

When teaching the horse the baby-give, it may take an average of 1,500 repetitions on each side. It's better to work in sets of one hundred before changing to the opposite side. It takes approximately seven minutes to get one hundred baby-gives. When you first begin, it may take ten or twelve minutes to get one hundred gives. You really have to concentrate.

As you work on these, keep in mind that you simply cannot pick up on the rein too much and you cannot get your horse too "soft."

We begin with a lateral flexion exercise, which teaches your horse to give and to be supple in a horizontal direction. She will bend at the nose, jaw, neck, and finally shoulder, back toward her hindquarters. For this, we pick up a rein at a standstill and wait until the horse gives in the direction of the pull.

The mistake most riders make here is that when they pick up the rein, they want to release as soon as the nose goes over. You need to wait for the release until the give is in the direction of the pull. When you do release, it should be no heavier than the weight of the rein. Lateral flexions are a critical foundation exercise and you can expect to do two to three thousand repetitions on each side. Some horses take longer than others, but it is vital that the horse truly learns this lesson before moving on.

When it comes to giving, you have two main types of attitude you run into with horses. The first is the "I Don't Mind and Am Happy to Give!" and the second attitude is the "I Don't Care." The latter can take far more repetitions to learn the lesson, and the consistency and timing of your release becomes even more important. However, even the heaviest horses who are most resistant to pressure can and do learn this lesson with time and patience. Please keep in mind, though, that all horses learn by conditioned response and they are just as likely to learn negative behaviors as positive ones!

Montana was a huge quarter horse who came into training with me some years back. This horse resisted the bit more than any other horse I have ever come across. Was this natural? No. This horse had been taught to be heavy; he was taught to pull away and lean on the rein. Montana's owner had consistently released when he was leaning on the rein and bit. I watched her do it and knew exactly how it had happened. When I say heavy, I mean this horse would lean with well over fifty pounds of pressure. This was the only time I got blisters and aching hands from reining work, just from trying to maintain pressure until he gave even a fraction that I could reward. I was using both hands braced on the saddle to maintain the contact.

The first session where we worked specifically on the bit, I had to spend about an hour and twenty minutes maintaining the fifty-plus pounds of contact before he released for the first time. Most of the time, it rarely takes more than twenty minutes before the horse gives that first key release. But Montana had been taught that he was supposed to be leaning; that he would get the release when he pulled. So that first session he was doing everything he thought was right: leaning, leaning, leaning. He was waiting for *me* to give like had been done for him all along. In the end, it took about three days of one- to three-hour sessions to get Montana to truly change his understanding of giving to the bit. Then he became nicely light and responsive.

Once your horse is doing the lateral flexion work well at a standstill, you should then move on to doing the same exercise but at a walk, then work up to a trot, and finally a canter. The higher the gait at which you are doing the exercise, the slower your hand speed must be in asking for the give. Your goal is that your hand speed is such that the horse can feel the weight of the rein before he actually feels the contact of the rein. With fifty-pound leaners like

Montana, anchor your hand to the saddle as if it were a post. This means he will pull on himself (and you are less likely to get blisters!).

The next exercise to work on is vertical flexion, getting your horse to bend and be supple on her forehand vertically. Begin by going forward with a soft leg, using the lightest leg contact you can. After about fifteen feet, pick up on the inside rein while maintaining light contact on the outside rein until the horse flexes at the pole. And then soften your hand (release slightly) to acknowledge that the horse is doing well. Then do it all over again. The goal is that the horse stays flexed, giving and accepting the bit. When has he accepted the bit? When he is no longer resisting. Once the horse is doing very well on one side, change direction.

Now if you put light on a scale of one to ten, Montana ended up about a four. But Montana was an "I don't care" horse, and that's about the most you can expect. Whatever her attitude, the approach and the method are the same for either type of horse. You are seeking to develop a light, responsive horse, looking for a long neck muscle that bounces at the walk and trot, and a head that will give off center four to six inches. It is okay if they go further, but not so far that they break out at the front of the shoulder.

Charles and Phantom demonstrate exercises working on giving to the bit, beginning at a standstill.

Charles lightly picks up on the rein to ask for the yield.

As Phantom begins to yield, we see the poll lowered as well.

Soft and supple, Phantom continues to yield to very light contact.

Nearly there!

Great lateral flexion is achieved.

Expect some resistance while the horse is learning to yield to the bit. This photo shows asking for lateral flexion.

Resistance.

Holding for more advanced lateral flexion work (when your standards are increasing).

Holding (which means maintaining contact only—*not* pulling) until the horse gives or softens just a little.

Asking for vertical flexion.

Asking for and getting vertical flexion with just the slightest contact.

Contrast Montana with Arabians like my horse Tennyson, or Thoroughbreds; the "hot" horses tend to be more responsive to the rein. They have more energy, and with proper training that translates into their being very light. Montana was a very lethargic horse and thus less responsive in general. The principles are the same, though. If we want a lighter horse, we have to be careful. We have a tendency to pick up on the rein while giving, looking for contact. Light here means the weight of the rein and not the actual contact, and that's what your goal should be. Your horse is light when the response comes simply from feeling the weight of the rein and she yields to that pressure. It may take three to six weeks and thousands of repetitions. It is well worth the time you invest in these exercises, because there is nothing more enjoyable than working with a truly light horse.

Head throwing is one common problem that can arise during the exercises. If you find your horse is throwing her head a lot when you ask for a one-rein give or a vertical rein give, first make sure there is not a physical cause for the reaction, such as sore teeth. If the problem is behavioral, you *must maintain full contact* while her head is flipping about until she horse quiets, even if it's just for a tenth of second, and then immediately release to acknowledge the correct response. Then continue until the horse is consistently giving you what you want. Your horse must learn that a quiet head will earn her the least pressure from you. Consistency is the key. Do *not* give up! This is very difficult and usually takes hundreds of repetitions before your horse will get even the tiniest clue.

MOVING THE HIPS OVER

Once your horse has begun to really understand giving to the bit, you will then begin work on training your horse to move her hips over. Lateral and vertical flexion are about getting the horse to begin to be supple on her forehand (the front half of the horse) and the next exercise starts to work with the horse's hindquarters, specifically to get the hips and hind legs to move on their own when cued. Not only does this exercise enhance your horse's lightness and responsiveness, but the act of moving the hips over for a one-rein emergency halt is the single greatest technique you can employ to stop a horse who is bolting or bucking. It can and has saved many people from terrible accidents.

Remember, you must have a solid go-forward cue established with your horse before beginning these exercises. Prior to starting these particular lessons, you should have taught your horse to laterally bend both right and left and to display vertical flexion (breaking at the pole at the first vertebrae). If you have a green horse, I recommend starting these exercises in a round pen or a small corral. These exercises teach any horse to be very focused on precues (lightness, disengaging the hips, and turning on the forehand). While these exercises are critical to gaining important control over your horse, especially when she's in flight mode or very emotional, they also can make a difference in your horse's responsiveness.

A client of mine, Joyce, brought in for training a real sweet Paint mare named Sienna. This mare was about ten years old and 15.2 hands. She had been to several trainers and was being shown regularly for English and Western Pleasure. This horse had a very good mind. She was extremely willing, but she was not responsive. While she was doing well in the show ring, her stops were not there, her head was too low, and she was far too much on the forehand. She was not performing to her potential. She needed to learn to give to the bit, yield at the hip, and respond to nice, soft cues.

So for Sienna's training program, we began with the basic foundation work we have covered previously. For Sienna, though, the key training exercises began when we worked on moving the hips over followed by stopping and backing.

To start with moving her hips over, I asked Sienna to go forward at the walk. Then working with one rein (it makes no difference which side you start with), I put my left leg on the horse where I wanted to teach her the cue would always be and picked up one rein to ask for the give. Instead of releasing (either the leg or the rein) when she started to yield, I continued picking up the rein, bringing her nose diagonally across her shoulder and maintaining the pressure until her hips began to move over or even if she leaned her hips. I released the second she gave me the tiniest yield. Then I moved her out forward once more and did it all over again. I repeated this exercise perhaps a dozen times before

Charles and Tennyson demonstrate the basics of the one-rein stop.

If the horse moves her hips over for you, It's very hard for her to be doing much else (like bolting, bucking, or rearing).

During an emergency one-rein stop, maintain contact until the horse's energy is released and she stands quietly for you.

I started looking for a more notable hip movement before I released. As we continued with the repetitions, I looked for greater hip movement before releasing the pressure.

Your goal is to eventually not have to make contact on the rein. When you pick up the rein, your horse will move her hips over. The leg on the correct area becomes a precue so your horse will begin to respond to just the precue. The horse learns to anticipate what is next and responds accordingly to avoid the pressure. Conditioned response is a wonderful thing.

This same basic technique can become a lifesaver when your horse is very excited or out of control. Picking up on two reins when a horse is out of control does not help—this only captures the horse's energy and actually fuels the horse's desire to flee. By picking up on one rein to have the horse move her hips over, you actually deplete the energy and give it someplace to go. It becomes a constructive exercise. To prepare for situations where you may lose control of your horse, I recommend practicing this at a walk, trot, and then finally a canter in preparation for one day when it could help you be safe.

STOPPING

Once you have mastered moving the hips over, it is time to teach your horse to stop and back up. With Sienna, I asked for a go-forward at the walk. Then I asked for the stop by picking up on both reins, and the instant I felt her feet stop, I released the rein for moment and then picked it back up and ask the feet to move backward. If the horse leans back even a little, release the pressure immediately as the reward. To help establish strong precues, I like a forward seat off the horse's back; it allows her to back more freely. I use a deep seat for my halt or whoa. To establish your precues, deepen your seat prior to asking the horse for a halt (which you can do just by dropping your heel in the stirrups) and then give the verbal cue (halt or whoa); only after that should you use the rein. This is about teaching a horse to be light and responsive. By using a consistent series of cues (with the final cue using the most pressure), you will teach your horse to learn to become lighter and lighter to avoid the pressure.

It's very important in backing to get the feet to move freely. Go forward, ask for the stop, and when the feet stop moving, release for a quick moment as a reward. Then pick back up on the reins and ask her feet to move back. After six to a dozen repetitions, you should look for more before you release. Look for two steps back before releasing; continue with this progression for a while. Then expect three steps before releasing and continue to build from there. Your goal with backing up is that your horse should be moving her feet so freely that it appears as if she is wearing Rollerblade in-line skates.

What we *never* want to do is to pull back on the horse's mouth or lean back in our shoulders. This causes the horse to raise her head and also hollows out the back.

If you run into difficulties getting your horse to back, here are a few tips that may help. Once the stop is completed, put an encouraging leg on the horse and as she takes a step forward, pick up the reins. When she takes a step back (or again, even leans back) immediately release the pressure (both rein and leg aid) to reward the behavior and let her know she is headed in the right direction. Then immediately do it again. You will find yourself repeating a pattern of pressure on–pressure off, pressure on–pressure off. As long as you are apply and release the pressure at the right times, within a short time your horse should understand what you are asking and quickly comply.

The exercise is complete when you barely pick up on the reins and the horse glides backwards. It can take two to four weeks to get these results.

Two more quick tips to help promote the backing action. First, if your horse locks up rather than backs, you can loosen one rein and pick up a bit more on the other, moving the hips over to unlock the feet. Once the hips are moving over and the feet are traveling, pick up on the rein again to ask for the back. The second method is to offset the rein when you back up, which will cause the nose to tip in about two to three inches. This also helps reduce the inclination of the horse wanting to rear.

Whatever it takes, once you get the horse backing, always make sure you release at the correct time and ask for more slowly. Be sure the horse understands the lesson before you attempt to ask for more. Over time you will find that your horse develops a wonderful, smooth backing glide and that she is far more responsive to both leg and rein cues. As an added bonus, we discovered that these exercises were so effective in getting Sienna to be so light and responsive that we were able to transition to riding her bridleless.

Charles demonstrates the basics of backing:
no resistance, poll-lowered, smooth movement.

SHOULDER CONTROL

In our previous exercises, we gained control over the jaw, pole, neck, ribcage, and hindquarters. Now we need to work on gaining control of the shoulder. This allows us to ask our horse to turn on her haunches, to do spins, and with hip control, to open gates, perform leg yields, pick up the correct leads, and do flying lead changes.

When we first started working on giving to the bit, we established the horse going forward in a nice circle, bending and softening from the neck down through the shoulder. To work on shoulder control, we are now going to expand on that exercise. We want the horse going forward with a nice bend through the body. At this point, if you encounter any resistance, *do not attempt this exercise.* The go-forward and bend must be relaxed and consistent. Upon encountering resistance, spend some time isolating the problem and then go back to the exercises designed to address that particular issue. We are trying to build a strong foundation not a house of cards. Do not move on to the next step until you have the solid blocks in place.

First, establish a twelve- to fifteen-foot clockwise circle with a nice go-forward and a soft bend. Next, add some inside leg while opening your right leg and right rein as a door for the horse. Now ask the horse to use that door with the inside leg and rein to take one or two steps over. Look for the nose to come toward the point of the shoulder. You may need to bump with your inside leg (not the spur), to get the reaction you want, which is one or two steps. Keep bumping until you get that step or two. You may experience resistance in the jaw since this is a new maneuver. Simply maintain your rein aids until the jaw gives and then release momentarily before continuing in the direction of the circle you started with.

For example, for bending in a fifteen-foot circle to the left, we ask the horse to move her shoulder to the right and then finish going left on the circle. There is an important reason to always resume the circle immediately after the release. If we always pick up on the rein and ask the shoulder to move over, the horse will learn to bleed out the shoulder. This means that instead of the shoulders being balanced as you move forward, one shoulder will lean sideways. Finishing off the exercise of going to the left (or the right for right directional circles) rather than ending with the release helps to ensure that the horse does not learn to bleed out the shoulder. This is important since you need your horse to be balanced to optimize performance and responsiveness.

As you progress, you will likely find that the shoulder starts leading farther than the hips. At this point, start thinking of the shoulders and hips as a set of speakers. When listening to music, we always want appropriate balance in our speakers and it's up to us to adjust the dials. Because we have already taught the horse to turn on the forehand, we can use this technique to help the hip catch up with the shoulder and then release only when the shoulder and hip are working together. This is a great suppling exercise. You can do this on the trail and it is especially effective coming back downhill because you have gravity working for you. You can do a leg yield to the right, change reins, and do a leg yield to the left. Next thing you know, you look like a drunken sailor coming down hill. At least you'll look like a drunken sailor with a very supple horse!

The next exercise to work on will be counter-arc bends. Again, start out with a soft clockwise circle. Next, open your right rein as if you are going to ask the shoulder to move over, but continue to ask the horse to move to the right. You will be creating a new circle with the shoulder leading to the right but with the horse's nose and head bent slightly to the outside (left). You will want to build on this until you can do a complete circle with the horse maintaining this posture. Not only does this soften the shoulder and increase your control; it also nicely establishes a supporting rein, which means that if you are riding a regular circle and the horse starts to bulge out at the shoulder, the right rein can support the shoulder from going out.

These exercises for shoulder control are important if you have a horse who drops her shoulders, a dangerous habit that makes it easy for a rider to fall out of the saddle.

A horse I worked with a few years back is a great example of a shoulder dropper. Linda, one of my clients, brought in a quarter horse named Schmidt. Schmidt was a sorrel gelding a bit over sixteen hands. Nice horse; good mind. No real issues except for one. Schmidt was the most radical shoulder dropper I have ever worked with. It was to the point that when you were cantering down the long rail to make a turn, he dropped his shoulder so bad that you felt like you were going to fall off him. If you did not have a good seat when this happened, you would likely hit the ground.

With Schmidt we did the following shoulder control exercises extensively. First, a left circle at the walk, making sure he was soft, consistent, and yielding before doing the circles to the right. Once he was solid in both directions, we did the same thing but at the trot, and then finally the canter. Next, we did this same exercise but in a square pattern, enforcing the shoulder control at sharp, ninety-degree turns. Again, working in one direction at the walk until every turn was consistent and then doing the exercise in the opposite direction. Finally, we took the exercise to the next level by working in a hexagonal pattern. A tip for novice riders: always look in the direction that you want to turn

Charles and Tennyson demonstrate positioning with counter-arc bend exercises. As you practice these (as shown in this series), you will see great improvements in how soft and supple the horse becomes.

Showing more flexibility.

Soft and responsive for the counter-arc.

before you actually ask for the turn. Swiveling your head and shoulders even subtly in preparation for a turn becomes a precue for your horse. Your horse will feel these shifts in your body position. When the precues are done consistently, your horse will learn to respond to them.

We were able to fix about 90 percent of Schmidt's problem within the first thirty minutes. By going back to basics when we needed to reestablish shoulder control with Schmidt, we solidified all his other cues as well. Once we accomplished this, we had a nicely balanced horse who was also upright. With a balanced and upright horse, you can begin working on transitioning up and down between different gaits.

ENGAGEMENT

Up to this point, I have been focusing quite a bit on horses who have had problems related to their personalities, past training issues, or their emotional and mental makeup. These are frequent sources of problems. But problems also arise due to the *physical* aspect of a particular horse. The good news is that within reasonable expectations, foundation training can also help solve problems relating to conformation.

Lexi is a seven-year-old quarter horse mare who belongs to my daughter-in-law. This horse is well trained and has a wonderful mind. We use her for lessons and she is a terrific all-around horse. So what's her problem? Well, Lexi is naturally built downhill, which means that her withers are set lower than her hips. This physical conformation (also known as "hip high") makes it difficult for a horse to engage and leaves her with a tendency to lean on the forehand. So what is engagement and why is it important?

Engagement involves training a horse to shift from front-wheel drive into rear-wheel drive. Engagement allows a horse to drive herself with her most powerful engine: her rear legs and hindquarters. When this occurs, the horse starts to carry herself. The more a horse is trained to engage, the deeper and more complete the engagement becomes. We can expect better performance because more engagement equals more horsepower. Zoom! (Okay, enough with the car analogies.) In short, we want the horse to use her hindquarters far more than her forehand.

Engagement is a level of control that we must have for any performance activities: sliding stops, flying lead changes, and even trail riding in the hills. You cannot get maximum performance unless your horse is using the strongest part of her body. Engagement also helps protect the horse from injury. Lameness is most common in the forequarters, so the more the horse uses the rear legs, the better. Whether you ride competitively, have working ranch horses, or ride the family trail horse, everyone should have the goal of getting their horses to engage well.

In the last sections we covered stopping, backing, moving the hips over, and basic shoulder control. We are now ready to work on teaching the horse to turn on the forehand, which is a more advanced tool we use to control the hips. The end goal is to gain reliable control over every part of the horse's body, which leads to exceptional performance. We need control of the hips for lateral work, side passes, opening gates, lead changes, engagement, and much more. We also need control of those hips for safety.

If your horse is bucking, bolting, spooking, or otherwise out of control, picking up on two reins does not help. As mentioned before, this only captures the energy and fuels the horse's bucking, etc. By picking up on one rein to have the horse move her hips over, you deplete the energy and give it somewhere to go. It is incredibly difficult for a horse to buck, bolt, or otherwise be out of control when you are moving her hips over. The one-rein emergency stop (which does require practice and training, as discussed earlier) could save your life one day.

Since Lexi had a hard time with engagement because of her physical conformation, I began working with her intensely to teach her to turn on the forehand. I asked her to walk forward and put my left leg back on her where I wanted the precue to be. Keep two things in mind about the leg. First, it is important to find the same spot to make the contact, since the leg on the horse becomes the precue for asking the hips to move over. Second, apply light contact only with the leg. Don't kick or apply much pressure—just light contact. The precue must be done first and be done consistently for the horse to make the association.

Once I had the leg on, I slowly picked up the left rein and added two to three pounds of pressure. I released the instant I felt her hips move over. Then I got her going forward again and repeated this exercise. After six to twelve repetitions on the same side, I was looking for Lexi to be moving her hips over *and* giving to the rein, which is what kept her light and responsive. My goal was to reach the point where Lexi would move off my leg while I was barely making contact with the rein, recognizing the leg contact as a precue and responding to that in order to avoid the pressure from the rein.

As I continued this exercise over time, Lexi became lighter and lighter, fluidly moving her hips over at the slightest contact of my leg. You must do this exercise on both sides of the horse. First I did the left side at the walk; then the right side at the walk. Then left side at the trot, right side at the trot, and finally moved on to the canter. Never move on to the next level until both of you have fully mastered the previous level.

If the horse locks up, use both legs to ask for the go-forward without releasing or changing the pressure on the one rein. As soon as you feel an attempt to move the hip, release all pressure on the rein and your legs. Then do the exercise repeatedly.

It is critical that the hindquarters are moving over until the horse yields to the bit. The horse will become heavy if you release when there is still contact. Once you have mastered this (and the exercises from the previous sections), you have control of the shoulder area through the hips.

Because we now have gained control of the hips through the leg aid, we can start motivating the horse to engage. This exercise encourages the use of the hindquarters rather than forcing the activity. There are signs to look out for that show your horse is starting to engage. The legs start coming up further, the stride becomes longer, the croup starts dropping, and finally we begin to see elevation in the withers! Depending on the conformation of the horse, you can achieve a *quarter-inch to three-quarter-inch correction*. In Lexi's case, her conformation has become nearly balanced; it's at least an 80 percent improvement. Now make no mistake—this does take time. It is a physical change. With Lexi, it took from four to six weeks to see a notable difference and extended time to achieve major improvement. But we did accomplish this and so can you. Foundation training can significantly improve the conformation and the performance. The real bonus is that you gain exceptional control and responsiveness at the same time.

TRANSITIONS

Transitions are a fantastic training tool. Whether a walk-to-trot transition, halt-to-trot transition, walk-to-canter transition, or any of the downward transitions, you cannot do too many transition exercises. Our goal is to teach the horse to receive transition cues from our seat and to use the rein as a last resort. Transitions also establish half halts, which greatly help horses with collection, and teach them to engage. Best, perhaps, is the mental training horses get with transition exercises; they really learn to listen to your seat and leg cues. If you have a horse that is too forward, performing halt-to-trot and then trot-to-halt transitions really helps engage their minds and focus on you while getting them to slow down.

We have reviewed exercises that give us control over *all* the major parts of the horse: jaw, pole, neck, shoulders, ribcage, and hindquarters. Let's now put these into action with a set of change-of-direction riding exercises designed for more advanced transition work. It's a great opportunity to use multiple cues and coordinate the control and movement of your horse's major body parts. As always, I recommend using a snaffle for these training exercises.

For this transition exercise, we will be working in a circle. Depending on the size of the horse, I prefer working in a fifteen- to twenty-meter circle. When doing circles, we always want to be keeping the horse slightly bent to the inside. If you have been practicing your gives, the horse should yield nicely and this next exercise should not be a problem. You may want to practice your basic circle work for a few minutes first as a warm-up before the transition work. Once you have the nice bend and response you want, you can begin these exercises.

Start your circle at a nice forward walk, and I mean a real "go someplace, working" kind of walk. At this pace, you will develop your fifteen- to twenty-meter circle. Once you've established the circle, you will then change direction by finding the *center of your circle* and passing through the center. As you pass through the center, change reins (you should be working on a loose rein, or, as some say, "on the buckle") and then change direction. This is like a serpentine exercise except you are changing direction. For example, if you are going left, turn to the center in a nice arc; go into the center and then go out in the new direction. The idea is to get the horse's body aligned, with the shoulders behind the head, the hips behind the shoulders at a slight arc. You don't want to see any more than a quarter or so of the horse's eye on the circle as you are doing this. Being able to see more of the eye will indicate you have too much bend happening.

Once you are doing this consistently at the walk for several laps (perhaps two to ten laps), you should then begin to ride her at the trot. Either a sitting or rising trot is fine. The goal now is to incorporate a transition into the exercise. When you change direction through the center, begin by relaxing your seat and lengthening your leg, which will allow your seat to come down. The rein should be the last thing you pick up if the horse has not *already* transitioned down to a walk.

If the horse resists transitioning down to the walk, begin circling down to a tight circle until she is forced (by physics) to break into a walk. Then find your center again, pass through, and go right back to your exercise at the trot again.

The reason we circle down to the walk is to get the horse to start listening to your seat as the primary cue. You should not have to pull on the reins. If you are consistent in circling down, she will figure it out within five to twenty minutes.

Once you are doing this well for both walk-to-trot and trot-to-walk transitions, you can advance to trotting through the center and asking the horse to move out into a canter. If you do your serpentine properly, when you go to the left ask for the canter with the right leg and put the horse into position to take the correct left lead.

You should now do one complete circle and then transition down with a deep seat and by dropping your heels. If she fails to transition down off these cues, go ahead and spiral down to smaller circles until she breaks into a trot. Once this happens you should again find your center, pass through the center, and change reins to the opposite direction.

Not only is this a great transition exercise; it really teaches your horse to listen to your seat and further enhances her ability to bend beautifully. It allows you to put the different parts you need that control your horse (jaw, pole, neck, ribcage, and hindquarters) and get all those parts *working together* for you. While you want your horse "listening to your seat" for a huge number of reasons, it really comes back to the key element of control.

In addition to all the benefits you gain for both showing and pleasure-riding purposes, this is also a very important problem-solving exercise for horses that are "too forward." Being too forward can be a huge problem. Many riders may try to deal with slowing down a "charging" horse by using a lot of rein. The problem with this is that without the proper technique and foundation, you end up putting a lot of pressure on the horse. This may actually raise her emotional level, make her flight instinct kick into gear, and result in her speeding up. This is a common problem with off-the-track Thoroughbreds (OTTB). For whatever reason, I meet a lot of green and novice riders who decide to get an OTTB as their first horse. Don't get me wrong, I love Thoroughbreds—they are super-responsive horses. But they are typically one of the more emotional horse breeds. The "go" button can get stuck in the on position for horses who have been trained to race, and that's a tough problem for the novice horse person to deal with. It's tough enough for experienced horse people!

I actually work with a lot of OTTBs, but one horse who really comes to mind as a great example is a huge OTTB named Winston. He was a gorgeous animal, a true black gelding who was easily seventeen hands. He came in for reschooling when he was about seven. Like a lot of OTTBs, he was too forward for his rider. He wanted to zoom everywhere during his rides, always moving out at full speed. His owner, Rita, had a hard time keeping control over him. She was not a bad rider, but her inability to slow him down had really shaken her confidence. And of course the more timid a rider gets, the more the problems can pile on.

With Winston, we spent time doing the basic foundation work that we have already covered. This got him to a point where he was nicely supple, and, more important, he was now listening to us and looking for the cues. I knew the transition work would be key for getting him to slow down and pay attention to his rider.

Largely because of all the prior work we had done with him, within about thirty minutes of doing these change-of-direction and transition exercises, he was already starting to relax considerably with a very nice trot and canter. Because of the transition work, there was no resistance at the bit and he was learning to take the correct lead. Going through the center of the circle and asking for the lead before the circle does kind of force the horse to take the correct lead. Ninety-nine percent of the time, you can do simple lead change work by doing every half circle and then picking up on the opposite lead. This is like a figure eight, which is also preparation for flying lead changes and a great exercise to do to prepare for true serpentine work. We do serpentines because they ask the horse to bend and soften the body and they teach balance. And it really helps get horses off their front end for transitions.

Severine works with Lexi on walk-trot transitions. Here she is in the trot.

Harder to see in a photo, but she is actually shifting her weight down, getting heavier in the saddle, which tells her horse to transition downward.

So that she achieves a nice soft walk only from using her seat aids.

Once you have mastered these exercises while riding with a light rein, you can then begin to use more connection with the rein and can start seeking collection, our next topic!

COLLECTION

We have carefully built upon a series of foundation training exercises that I use with every horse—exercises that allow you to gain control over the emotional, mental, and physical aspects of the horse; exercises that promote having a horse that is extremely light, supple, and beautifully responsive. All of these exercises help us achieve one critical goal no matter what discipline you ride: collection!

Collection is and should be a primary end goal for every rider. I'm sure you hear people taking frequently about how to get their horse collected, and the importance of collection to their own pursuits. Why is that? What is collection and why is it so vital for every rider?

Speaking in strictly physical terms, collection happens when the horse can compress her body. She brings the rear toward the front, and the body and withers are raised up. The hind legs are extended up under her, while the croup is dropped. She drives herself not only with her legs, but primarily with her hindquarters. She will have a nice rainbow arc in her neck and will be on the bit with her face perpendicular to the ground.

Mentally and emotionally, collection occurs when the horse is truly listening to you. She understands all your cues and is able to coordinate all the key parts of her body that you have been working on gaining control over into a very powerful, balanced, and fluid movement.

What you gain with a collected horse is better performance in every gait with far greater impulsion. Collection allows you to excel at leg yields, spins, turnarounds, flying lead changes, collected trots, and canters—just a better performance no matter what you are asking the horse to do. Collection means the horse is using herself 100 percent and you are 100 percent in harmony with your horse.

All the work we have been doing has been leading up toward collection. We must have control over all the major body parts: jaw, pole, neck, shoulders, ribcage, and hindquarters. We must have acceptance of the bit—and not at ten pounds of pressure either—ideally, you are riding a horse with the weight of the rein only on the bit. If the horse is heavier than that on the bit, she will be heavy on the forehand, and thus it will be impossible for you to get true collection.

As a trail rider, you also need collection. Going up and down hills efficiently requires collection. The extra impulsion you gain from driving from the rear means you can go farther and that you can go better (more efficiently for your horse). This means a better heart rate for your horse, which is critical for endurance riding. A horse who can be collected is a fit horse. The body has been conditioned physically, the top line is strong, and the horse is balanced from a profile point of view. This means there is a straight line from the front end to the back—not tilted, with equal weight on each end.

We gain collection through a series of exercises that show what we want: haunches in, shoulders in, leg yields, walking pirouettes, teaching a horse to turn on the haunches, and teaching a horse to shift her weight back to her hindquarters. The horse must know her go-forward cues and what all your leg cues mean. Then the rein simply acts as the final method of communication. Think of the bit as a dam gate; we can let so much energy go out through the nose or else capture it and transfer that energy up through the withers.

For example, we had a show horse, Mariah, come in for training. Mariah was so heavy on the forehand, it was impossible to get her to pick up the correct lead. As a result, we could not do flying lead changes. Now, Mariah was not what folks would consider a problem horse. She was about nine years old, a super-cooperative mare with no emotional issues at all. She had been professionally trained years before and then spent a long time being worked by amateur competitors. But her training had degraded over the years because her riders had not maintained the performance standards.

With Mariah, we went back to the basics to get control of all her key body parts, to get her to be responsive to aids, and to end up with a horse that was very light and supple. With time and patience, Mariah discovered there was another world out there other than being heavy on the forehand 60 to 70 percent. When we started working her, she had big shoulders, a puny hind end, no top line, and her neck was inverted (muscles on the bottom and skinny on top), kind of U-shaped. In about three to four months with a good diet, all the great gymnastic exercises we do as part of the foundation training regiment and conditioning training, we ended up with a horse who learned to pick up her correct leads (both right and left) and to do exceptional lead changes. All because we collected this horse and got her to pay attention.

While there is not a quick fix to getting a horse collected, it is critical that collection is one of your most important goals with your horse. Collection comes from thorough training on all three aspects of your horse: emotional, mental, and physical. Collection results from your consistency and commitment to meeting and raising the expectations for performance from both your horse and yourself as her rider and trainer. Collection is achieved through solid, systematic foundation training. That is something that everyone really can do with their horse. *It only makes all the difference in the world!*

TRAINING BABIES

I want to add to our exercise work a discussion on training foals and youngsters. Every year I meet horse owners who have gotten or are considering getting a foal for the first time. Many people like the idea of raising their own horse and getting "everything right." There is a natural appeal in having a horse who is your very own from the start, a horse who will love you more than anyone else, a horse who will not buck, bolt, rear, or kick; a horse you can raise properly to avoid any major issues. Finally, a horse that's your own perfect dream horse, all because you raised her yourself.

Foundation Training and the Foal

After years of having clients come to me for help after getting a foal, I would like to share some of my thoughts. First, it is much harder work than anyone expects and frankly, much of it can be tedious. Seemingly simple things like leading, tying, picking up feet, and bathing are not always easy to teach babies. In many cases, the most fundamental lessons can be the hardest to teach. Until they learn these basic skills, there is little of the more fun activities that you can do with foals. Not only can halter training be difficult, but hoof trimming and vaccines can become a true nightmare as well.

Yes, babies are adorable. When they are in the right mood, being all cute and fun, you will feel all sappy, happy, and silly. But there will be the other times, when you ask them to do something they do not want to do and they might charge, rear, bite, kick, or most commonly, just plain refuse. Those times can be awful and even dangerous.

If you do decide to get a youngster, never buy one on a whim. Getting a baby is a huge responsibility and you should make a detailed plan, from where you are going to keep her to how you will train her. Always plan to get a foal well in advance and be as prepared as possible. Some of the ways to be prepared include:

- **Videos.** Watch groundwork and handling videos over and over again. Whether it's one of my *Ground Manners and Leading* videos or another trainer's video about halter breaking, watch as many as possible to see how training lessons are broken down into tiny patterns of pressure and release responses and think about how you could break that step down even more.

- **Hands-on work.** Find an apprenticeship program or some type of work or lessons with a trainer or breeder who handles foals regularly. Get lots of supervised hands-on practice before you get your own foal.

- **Hire your own trainer.** There is nothing wrong with asking for help. If you are going to get a baby, be willing to set aside your ego, if needed, to ensure that you are doing the right thing by your foal.

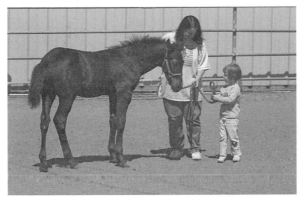

Sometimes the hardest thing you can do is to resist getting a foal in the first place.

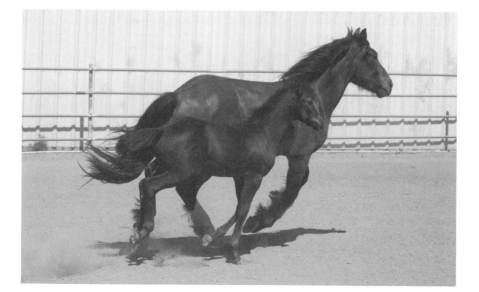

Once you have a foal, what should you do with her for the first couple years of her life before she's ready to saddle? As much as possible! While this does not mean your foal needs to be "in training" for the first twenty-four or thirty-six months of life, it does mean that you can and should start foundation training. You do need to remember to be sensitive to growing bones (and short attention spans!), so none of these lessons should be long or intense, but there is no reason you cannot teach all of the foundation training exercises I outlined up to the point we began giving to the bit under saddle. All the groundwork before that is perfectly suitable for babies of any age. Again, just keep the sessions short and very focused on small, simple steps to make progress. If done right, you will end up with a sound, focused horse who should be a easy transition to saddle when ready.

Training a Baby for Veterinary and Farrier Work

One of the things we cannot wait too long to do is to get the foal trained to accept a vet or farrier. I'll cover this as an additional training issue since I get questions about this all the time and it's important for successful initial visits. Horses have very good situational memories, so a bad first experience with the vet or farrier can be hard to overcome. Whether you are getting ready for the first visit or overcoming problems with work done earlier, the foundation steps are the same. The only difference may be how much time you have to spend on each lesson.

The primary goals are straightforward. Your horse needs to accept being touched everywhere on the body and to have that contact be done by a stranger. All of these requirements represent significant pressure, especially to a young horse. So while it may seem like not such a big deal, these can actually be tough milestones to accomplish. These are key cornerstones in your horse's foundation training and you should approach them with a careful planning, a lot of patience, and above all, that magic word, consistency.

Before you begin to work on these training exercises, you need to ensure you have already done the necessary work to prepare your horse to giving to pressure without resistance. The horse needs to be soft on a lead line and while lunging, to have solid go-forward and stop cues, and to tie well. Once these are accomplished, you can move on to the work below.

The first step is getting your horse to accept being touched anywhere on her body. For most owners, this is actually a fun and rewarding training exercise. It's a great way to bond with your horse. Like tying, this is very straightforward. It may just take time and patience depending on how fearful or resistant to pressure your horse is. Begin by discovering where your horse is the most comfortable being touched. Spend lots of time grooming and rubbing that area and slowly expand your zone. One tip: most horses love having the base of their mane and around their withers massaged. You'll notice that this is often where horses nibble and rub each other.

If your horse begins to pull away or resist when you touch her, do not back away! Stay with her, maintaining the contact until she releases and relaxes, even for just a second; then you release the pressure. The important exception to this rule is when you are at risk of getting hurt or are in danger. Other than presenting a safety risk, rewarding the horse by stopping the contact when she resists trains her to resist. Conduct lots of short sessions with your young horse in which you spend time grooming and touching her all over, always ending when you see significant improvement. Work on the legs last (since they can be a more dangerous area) and concentrate on getting your horse very relaxed when being touched. Make sure you work on every area of the body, especially the head, ears, mouth, stomach, and for those who will be doing sheath cleaning, well, you know what you have to do.

When you are ready to start on the legs, work with a dressage whip, first using it as an extension of your hands. This provides extra distance as a safety measure; you will be able to tell how sensitive the horse is and if she is liable to kick. Use the end of the whip as you would a hand and touch the horse all over the legs and stomach using the same pressure and release techniques; that is, maintain that contact until she gives. When she seems relaxed with the contact, you can work with your hands. Firmly move your hands down each leg, spending plenty of time on each section. Do not ask the horse to lift the hoof. If she does so on her own, fine. But for now focus only on the contact. When you go to work on the back legs, make sure the horse is relaxed while you are standing behind her and at her side and ensure your head can't be kicked.

Now I hear all the time, "Well, I can touch my horse anywhere but my vet can't get near her." Chances are you have not trained her to accept strangers. Remember, you have trained her to accept the pressure from you. Every new person will represent fresh pressure. So now you need to desensitize your horse to strangers. Start encouraging friends and other horse owners to groom and pet your horse. The more exposure she has to being touched by unfamiliar people, the better your vet and farrier visits will be. Just remember to always be safe and not ask too much of your horse. One tip I recommend, if your horse is at a facility where the vet and farriers visit regularly, ask them to stop by and briefly visit with your horse. Have them stroke, pet, and give verbal praise to help get your horse comfortable with them when she is not being worked on.

Ask your vet to schedule extra time for the first visit. If your vet is in a rush, the first visit is almost doomed to fail. Ask the vet to factor in time to let the horse acclimate to the vet and so as not to rush through anything, especially shots. Other things you can do include spending time early on getting your horse vaccinations ready. This can be a combination of poking and pinching at your horse's neck—not a lot and not too hard; what you are doing is simulating the brief sensation of the shots. Follow this with some extra massaging in that area to help desensitize the horse to the sensation. As a final step, move onto using a toothpick end. You can do some short jabs with a toothpick that do not break the skin, but do offer a very similar feel to the needle. Another good thing is to get a hypodermic syringe (without the needle) and show it to your horse a lot, moving it to her shoulder, followed by the toothpick. Likewise, for worming, you can buy a plain oral syringe, put a little apple juice in it and regularly practice putting the oral worming syringe in your horse's mouth. You can also put a small plastic tube briefly in your horse's nose to prepare her for the nasal strangles vaccine. When available, ask your vet to combine shots rather than doing a series of several injections.

The approach for getting ready for the farrier is similar. Once your horse is comfortable with all the physical contact, you can work on getting her to pick up her feet. I see two common mistakes people make to teach this to their horses. First, they ask their horses too soon to pick up their feet too high and for too long. Second, they tend to rush through this training. Remember, these are prey animals with a serious flight instinct. When they are giving you their feet, they are giving up their ability to run. That's asking a lot of them, so take your time. Start by asking for the feet to be up only an inch or so off the ground and only for a second or two. When you can get that from all four feet, ask for a few seconds longer but still keep the feet very low. First, build on the duration of holding the hoof up low, and then over time you can bring the hoof higher as well. And again, try not to release if the horse is resisting. I know it's hard but you want to release when she is giving the hoof and relaxed. That is one reason why it's very important to start with short asks and make it easy for her. Once she is comfortable with having her hooves held up both longer and higher than the farrier will want, get yourself a rasp to practice moving across the hoofwall. You do not need to trim her; this will just begin to get her used to a strange feel and sound around the feet. Run the rasp back and forth a lot and tap the hooves with the metal. It is important for you to try to make more noise and contact than the farrier normally would to get her used to the extreme limits of the experience. As with the first vet visit, ask your farrier to allow for plenty of extra time for the first trim visit. You have to be patient with a young horse and stick with the basics until she is ready. If you try to rush her into it, you could have a lifetime of unpleasant farrier visits ahead.

If you do plan to raise a foal, start planning now to set up yourself and your baby for success. Just remember that baby steps takes on a whole new meaning when it comes to being patient and persevering. By starting them young with foundation training exercises in short work sessions, you are guaranteeing your-self a much easier start under saddle down the road as well as having a horse who is respectful, fun, and loving.

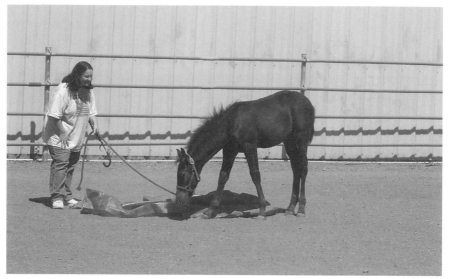

It's never too early to start foundation training with your foal or yearling!

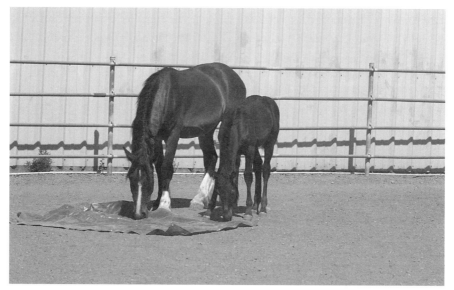

It's easy to integrate training elements into the daily routine with babies, like regular exposure to tarps while in paddocks.

Even playing with objects also doubles as great despooking work. Make it fun for both of you!

STARTING OLDER HORSES

I am frequently asked if there is a difference in how you start an older horse under saddle versus a youngster. This may mean an adult horse who has been left largely untouched in pasture until she's eight or ten years old, or adopting an adult BLM Mustang (wild mustangs are available from the federal Bureau of Land Management). Folks want to know what to do to successfully start an older horse.

There is not a difference in the *methodology*, but there will almost certainly be a need for a difference in the amount of *time* you spend and perhaps in the *application* of some of the training. In the most simplistic form, we can say that older horses are more set in their ways. Just as with people, we know children are generally more malleable than adults. They will give more quickly than adults, responding to elders as a natural respect relationship, in addition to the fact that they have not had as much time to build up habits and conditioned responses to various situations.

When we start a young horse, we get the benefit of the open mind and an easier time to train in the conditioned responses. Now we can (and do all the time) have that same success with an older or a wild horse, but it usually takes longer. In practical terms, this may mean that we plan on taking an extra two to three months in our training plan to get the horse well started under saddle. Is this required all the time with an older or wild horse? No, but it will be necessary for most of these horses.

Horses who have lived well into their adult life largely unhandled have much stronger socialization and herd behaviors. Wild mustangs tend to have a much higher fear instinct (flight button) than domesticated horses, since they are often still living as prey animals.

So you need to take many of the training steps even more slowly and will need to spend more time on despooking and desensitization exercises well before you climb into the saddle. Older and wild horses require tremendous patience, as well as consistency and persistence. While training any horse requires these characteristics, the older or wild horse will need even more for a successful transition into a safe saddle mount.

That being said, let me review the likely progression of exercises you would do to start one of these animals. All these exercises have been covered in detail already, so I'm providing a high-level overview of a typical training sequence.

1. Round pen exercises. If you have one available, the round pen is a highly effective tool to begin working on building respect with an adult horse. A round pen provides a safer area for you to work where you can use the horse's natural instincts with pressure and release to control their feet. Once you control their feet, you control their direction and space, which gives you the ability to capture the mind and really make a solid connection with you as the horse's leader.

2. Halter break. Next, you need to halter-break the horse. In practical terms, this means she must understand giving to pressure.

3. Line work exercises. If you do not have a round pen, or, as a next step after the round pen, line work (into which halter training comes into play) is the way to go. Start with basic change of direction work (and on a twenty-plus-foot line if with an initially dangerous animal), and get the go-forward cue to be 100 percent consistent in both directions. Get the horse to halt and look at you when asked.

4. Complex line work. From there you can work on landings and then move onto figure eights. Next, work on concentrated circles, reinforcing further the go-forward cue and getting control of the horse's nose, head, neck, shoulders, and hips to bend nicely around you in both directions.

5. Leading on a line. Another type of basic but critical line work concerns leading and respecting space. Your goal is to teach your horse that equivalent of the canine heel. Even though your horse has a halter on with the lead line in your hand, whenever you are leading her, there should be slack in the line and the horse should be walking just next to you. When you speed up, she should speed up. When you slow down or stop, she should too, cued just off your own body position. You should also be able to step away several feet from your horse and have her stand there. She should not crowd into you. It is fine to pet, hug, kiss, or generally love on your horse, but this should entail you entering her space to deliver the attention, not her entering into yours to demand it.

6. Sacking out. Next, I recommend sacking out your horse. Use any of the many despooking exercises we discussed or make up your own, as long as the work reinforces giving to pressure while the emotional level is high. Take time to install the kind of conditioned response buttons you will need later under saddle. When done well, groundwork alone has 70 percent to 80 percent carryover into the saddle. So while you are deliberately working on getting your horse's emotional level up, take the opportunity to make sure you can achieve the emotional control you need under saddle later.

7. Translating from ground to saddle. As part of the preceding exercises, you have already been getting the horse used to the equipment (bridle, bit, blanket, saddle). Once you are ready for your first rides, you must focus on translating the ground cues you have already taught into under-saddle cues. If you have been consistent in your cues, you will see that the horse is responsive and easy under saddle, even in the first few rides.

8. Work on basics in the saddle. Replicate the basics you established on the ground into the saddle time. Establish a solid go-forward, stopping, backing, moving the hips over, shoulder control, etc. You then begin to work on giving to the bit.

9. Giving to the bit. Giving to the bit will be among the most important things you can accomplish with your horse. You will likely have to do hundreds of baby-gives and gives until it becomes a true conditioned response. As part of this training, you will also be teaching her the very important one-rein stop and you'll be gaining control of the nose, head, neck, shoulder, and hips under saddle. Control under saddle will help get

you develop a light and supple horse, which is great for every discipline. You can work on turning on the forehand and getting the horse to step under herself and to use her hindquarters. That leads to engagement.

10. Teaching collection. Once the horse is truly engaged and uses her hindquarters to drive herself forward, then transitions and even collection become much easier to achieve. Then it just comes down to lots of miles and always raising the expectations for performance as you achieve each goal you set for yourself.

So how long does this take? There is no magic number. I get frustrated when I hear some trainers promise to start a horse in thirty to sixty days. Sure, you can *start* a horse in that amount of time, but owners often believe that translates into a "well-broke" animal. How long it takes to get a horse trained depends on the horse's personality, the horse's emotional level (how much she responds to pressure and release via her fear levels), the horse's maturity, and any trauma or baggage the horse may have in her background. It also depends on the knowledge, consistency, persistence, patience, and follow-through of the trainer.

Are there horses who are well-broke in short periods of time? Well, there are very complacent horses who are naturally responsive, and with a good trainer they may be pretty safe and decent in shorter periods. But they are definitely the exception.

Horses do not wear a watch. It takes as long as it takes for a given horse. It will generally take longer for an older or a wild horse. But if you have the time to invest, they can also be wonderful animals when finished and you do get the benefit sometimes of their extra mental maturity.

Be very methodical and patient if you are doing the training yourself, or seek out a very good trainer who will take the right time and approach needed for the individual animal.

We all look hard at the expense of starting a horse, but the reality is that it's a pittance compared to the cost of horse ownership over many years. More to the point, the cost of *not* starting a horse properly under saddle will be more expensive (hopefully not including hospitalization) than if you had spent a bit more upfront for more training months and/or a better trainer. Make the right decision before sending your horse out for training!

4

It's Never, Ever
the Horse's Fault

The majority of the training that occurs at my ranch involves "problem" horses. I became a foundation training fanatic and enthusiast when I discovered that it really does correct any problematic behavior, anything from the more dangerous issues such as bucking, bolting, spooking, buddy sour, trailer loading, pullback, etc., to more performance and competitive issues such as problems with engagement, flying lead changes, and collection. Foundation training eliminates the gaps that cause problem behaviors or poor performance.

Less than 10 percent of horse trainers specialize in working with problem horses. It's not because the horses are a problem, it's because the owner or handlers are often the problem. It may not be the current owner; the behavior could have been inherited. Regardless, the true problem resides with the human, not the horse. Unfortunately, we humans are far harder to train than any horses. Many of the good old boy horse trainers are often superb with the animals but may not have particularly strong "people skills."

When I say it's never, ever the horse's fault, I mean it—it really never is! Horses are what they are because of the three main aspects of their makeup—emotional, mental, and physical— and their natural instincts. If we fail to train them to behave or perform in a way they can understand and feel rewarded by, it's not their fault. With the exception of *maybe* two to three horses I have encountered in all my life who were clearly mentally imbalanced, every other problem horse I have encountered has come to me because of improper or inadequate training. But once the horse has a thorough foundation and has learned exercises that addressed the specific behavior, the horse no longer performed the problem behavior.

Look back at Allison's horse Bandwidth as an example. That horse bucked violently for every trainer for more than a year and half. I took a different approach than the other trainers and did what I always do. I spent several months doing nothing but thorough foundation training on that horse, making sure there were no holes in his training and teaching him emotional control. There was no "anti-bucking" lesson per se. But when I finally got on that horse's back to ride, there was no longer a bucking button on him. We had moved him away from the negative cue he learned somewhere along the way and, through conditioned response, had given him a new outlet for that emotional energy. But, should he get into the hands of someone who does not continue to maintain his emotional control work and communicate with him as he needs for confidence and stability, he may begin bucking again.

The thing to keep in mind is that the training is never finished. It always has to be maintained, and foundation is always the place you should return to.

When horses come to my ranch for training, extensive classes and instruction for the owner are included as part of the cost. If owners cannot or will not take the time and interest to attend the available lessons, then I not only abdicate responsibility for success after they go home, I may even suggest that they stop training with me. I can train the horse while he's with me, but the owner has the responsibility to become that horse's ultimate trainer on his or her own. The owner must learn how to maintain the horse's training. Each of us is responsible for communicating our standards and expectations to our horse in a way they can understand and respond to. The Ultimate Foundation Training is simply the method by which we apply exercises to control the mind, body, and emotions in a way they can understand. But again, the responsibility to get it right rests solely on our shoulders.

Problem horses are made, not born, and the problem usually arises from one or more of the following situations.

1. We purchase a horse who is not a good match for our skills, personality, or interests.

2. We are not mentally prepared to conduct effective horsemanship training.

3. We do not find the best resource if we come to the point that we need professional training help.

Let's talk about how to address these situations so you are successful.

BUYING THE RIGHT HORSE

While my foundation training program can certainly turn every horse into a light, responsive, and respectful animal, how much work and skill are needed to be successful will depend on the match between the owner (as his key trainer) and the horse. Horses do have various personalities, but it is up to us humans to change our personalities and communication styles to accommodate them. Depending on the type of horse we choose, this can be easy or difficult. For example, a timid human will have a much harder time with a bully horse but may thrive with a compliant one. If we do not take the time and patience to really find a good match between ourselves and the horse we select, it is certainly not the horse's fault when the relationship starts to go wrong.

Before you look at horses, take the time to think about what you want. What do you really want to do with this horse? Are you looking for a horse to keep for life, or one to build your confidence and skills on over time and then move on to a more advanced horse? Do you have any special dreams of showing or learning a specific discipline? Will you want to do more training with this horse? Does the horse need to be kid friendly, gentle, or very forward, and will conformation matter? Clearly define your goals for this horse.

Second, do the math. How much do you have to spend? Keep in mind that the horse's price will be peanuts compared to other costs over time. Training and health issues will be the largest factors. So when evaluating a horse, it is critical that you are able to judge if this horse will need additional training or health care. Create a budget that is realistic for you and family.

Third, resist the urge to feel rushed. Once you are ready to buy, you may want one *now*. But again, in most cases you are looking for a long-term, if not lifetime, equine partner. Unless you met and married your spouse right away, take a deep breath and be prepared to be picky. This is similar to marriage; the difference is that the bad ones often put you in the hospital rather than divorce court. Buy only when you find the absolute right horse.

Fourth, take all your friends' advice with a grain of salt. Unless you have a trainer whom you trust, you are going to get different advice from everyone on what to look for. You may have a specific breed, color, size, and even age in mind, and yet your absolute perfect dream horse could be totally different. Instead, focus on the three key aspects of the horse to determine suitability: emotional, mental, and physical.

The emotional aspect should be the most important area for a novice rider. The temperament, personality, and instincts of the horse are all hinged on the emotional level. The emotional level is also the hardest area to change. I believe that most novice riders, unless extremely confident with low fear levels, should seek out horses with low to average emotional levels.

The mental aspect of the horse is also very important. How willing is he to listen and focus on you? How quickly does he learn lessons? Does he like to work? Is he alpha (meaning the herd boss), submissive, or somewhere in the middle? Knowing his mental makeup can also help you determine if you are a good fit for each other. Remember that horses can't change their personality. It is up to us to adjust our communication styles for them.

The physical aspect is the hardest thing for the novice to judge. It's not only a question of health and soundness; the horse's conformation can also significantly affect its ability to excel in certain disciplines. You do not want to pay a vet to check every horse you consider, so it's helpful to be able to do a basic evaluation yourself. The biggest problem areas are usually the legs and hooves. The best thing to do is to find horse friends who have animals with splints, bowed tendons, founder, and other problems. Ask them to show you how to check out a horse for any warning signs. Also run your hands and fingers over the horse's neck, withers, shoulders, back, and hindquarters. See if you can detect any flinching or soreness. If you can't find anything, then you can further evaluate the horse.

Following is an evaluation checklist I recommend for horse buyers to follow:

- **Prior to the visit.** Ask the seller not to do anything with the horse that day until you get there. Find out exactly how often the horse has been worked in the prior week and what the work entailed. Plan on bringing a 12- to 20-foot lead line, lunge whip or dressage stick, blue tarp, stick with a plastic bag on the end, electric clippers, and any other items you think may be good for despooking work.

- **When you get there.** First ask the seller to halter the horse and lead to where he can be tied. How does horse accept halter? How does he lead? Then ask to leave horse tied up for five minutes to see how quietly he stands. Now ask to have the seller pick up all four feet, rub the horse's belly, pet the face, and touch the ears. Watch how the horse reacts to all of these. As long as horse seems fairly accepting of the contact, ask if you can groom the horse. Do a full grooming session and look for any sensitive spots. Next, pull out your electric clippers to see how the horse accepts the clippers around the muzzle and bridle path.

Now it's time for groundwork. Just in the halter, find an area where you can do some leading with the horse. Walk around the property a bit to test how heavy the horse is in hand. Does he walk ahead or behind? Is he spooking at anything? Does he seem attentive or very quiet? Does he stop when you stop? Will he back easily for you?

Then ask the seller if the horse works on a line. If yes, ask them to do some change of direction exercises for you at the walk, trot, and canter. Pay attention to where the horse's head, shoulders, and hindquarters are. Is he staying light on the lead line or pulling away? Is his head turned slightly inward to show focus on the handler; are his shoulders slightly bent in at an arc? Are his hindquarters out or coming into the handler? Is he moving forward with nice energy, or is he slow, or is he showing too much energy? Is he transitioning from walk to trot and cantering off verbal cues easily or does he need extra pressure (like a whip) to get him to transition? Is he staying with the gait as asked? Does he look "high" or more relaxed as the work continues? Look for lowered head, licking, and chewing. Any bucking, kicking, or bolting? Also take this time to watch for any signs of lameness. Look for any favoring of the hooves or dipping of the shoulder. Lameness can often appear working in one direction on lead but not the other, so keep your eyes open at all times.

Next, work the horse yourself on the line. Note any differences in the horse's performance working for you versus the seller. Do you feel comfortable asking the horse to go forward, transition, and stop? Is the horse paying attention to you? Is he reacting when you ask for something? If there is a round pen, take advantage of it. If the line work has been comfortable for you, take the horse into the round pen yourself and take the halter off. Ask him to move out with good energy. After a couple of laps, see if you can get the horse to do a change of direction. If the horse has not done a lot of round pen work, you will likely not get an inside turn, though you can try. The important thing is that either way you can get the horse to stop his feet and turn the other direction when you ask. Do frequent turn of direction exercises until you see the horse is really paying attention to you. If you see clear progress, it's a good indication he is at least willing. If there is not a round pen, just do more extensive line work. The emotional control checks I will discuss next can be done on line or in the ground pen.

Now get ready to test the emotional level of the horse. Begin with the blue tarp. Fold the tarp into a small square and approach the horse with it. Look for any aversion to the object; can you touch the horse with the tarp? Using pressure and release methods, take time to see if you can eventually put large sections of the tarp over the horse. Likewise, ask the horse to cross over the tarp while it is folded in a small square while doing change of direction work. If successful, slowly unfold the tarp into larger and larger portions to see how well the horse will cross the tarp. You can do similar tests with the plastic bag on a stick. These are simply the exercises discussed in the despooking section that allow you to assess the horse's natural fear level, and most importantly your ability to bring the emotions down once they have been raised. What you are looking for is not to see that the horse does not react at all, but rather how he reacts. Is he merely attentive, does he step back a little bit, or does he bolt like crazy? How well does he accept the pressure of these items? How long does it take to get him to accept the pressure? How quickly (if at all) can you get him to be relatively relaxed in the face of this new scary stuff? Your goal is to know what he does in the face of something unfamiliar and scary as his natural reaction.

Now ask the seller to tack up the horse. Watch how the horse accepts the bridle and saddle, especially the cinch. Watch for signs the horse is ridden with extra aids, such as tie-downs. If you see lots of extra equipment, ask why, and how the horse does without the equipment. Watch the seller do groundwork with the horse fully tacked up. Determine if the horse is not accepting the gear well or is more emotionally high under saddle and bridle.

Next ask the seller to ride the horse for you at the walk, trot, and canter. Ask for change of direction work while paying very close attention to how much pressure the horse needs to start, turn, and stop. How much leg is being used and how much contact on the reins? This is your chance to judge very carefully how responsive the horse is at his current state. This will tell you how much (if any) training you may need to invest in if you decide you want the horse. Also watch how the horse does transitions with a rider. Any signs of resistance or fear? Lots of green or emotional horses are fine at the walk and trot, but can really act out at the canter.

At this point you need to judge your own comfort level carefully. If you feel good about it, now is the time for you to ride the horse. If you don't, ask yourself why. Chances are your intuition is telling you that this is not the right horse for you. This does not mean you need to canter the horse. But if the horse seems appropriate for you, you should feel comfortable doing walk-to-trot work. It's important to feel for yourself how much contact the horse needs to respond from your leg, reins, and seat. What does the overall emotional level of the horse seem to be? Is he relaxed and focused or in some state otherwise?

Mounting comfort is also very important to evaluate. Does he stand still for the mounting and does he stand for a mounting block? Are his ears pinned way back as you mount? Can you feel him hunching up as you mount?

Next, after you are done riding, ask the seller if you can (weather permitting) rinse the horse off with a hose to get a feel for how he bathes and accepts water. The last thing in an evaluation is, if they have a trailer (or bring your own), try loading and unloading the horse several times to watch his reaction.

This includes closing the gate. Lots of horses load well and then may freak out when enclosed.

At this point you are done with the initial evaluation and should do one of the following four things:

1. Walk away because the horse does not feel right.

2. Ask to put down a refundable deposit, pending a vet check and second evaluation because the horse seems fantastic and you don't want to risk him being sold to someone else.

3. Ask to come back another day to work with the horse and ride again. You have some doubts but are not sure either way.

4. You love the horse but want a purchase trial agreement.

The best advice I can offer is always to try to get a purchase trial contract. A seven- to fourteen-day trial is a winning situation for everyone. The seller is protected by partial or full payment up front in conjunction with a clear contract with the buyer, and the buyer has the ability to spend time on their own territory taking the horse through his paces and really testing his disposition. Plus, being able to use one's own vet for the prepurchase eliminates any possible concerns of drugging.

What you risk as a buyer with a trial agreement is anything happening to the horse while in your care (you break it, you buy it), the cost of transporting the horse to your own facility (potentially both ways), the feed and care costs during that time, and then the costs of the vet check, which I usually do last. I make sure the horse has the emotional and mental makeup I want before paying for the prepurchase exam. As long as you are at a good facility, the horse trailers well, and you do not take undue risks during the trial, your exposure of ending up with a horse who is not suitable for you is quite low. Equine insurance is an option to alleviate some of those risks. The benefits of trying the horse out speak for themselves. I have included in this chapter a sample contract that may give you some ideas on how you would proceed as either a buyer with a trial agreement.

This is your chance to ensure you end up with exactly the partner you are looking for. Don't underestimate how important it is to find the right horse. Remember, it will be up to you to adapt to the horse, so make sure it is the relationship you are seeking. Take your time. Be thorough. Be selective. Be sure. And whenever possible, try before you buy!

Disclosure: This is a sample of a generic agreement from the State of California and is not appropriate for use in all situations. Please consult with an attorney to customize or create a contract suitable for your own situation. It is provided to serve as a sample reference guide only.

THIS AGREEMENT is made between _____, residing at _____, hereinafter referred to as SELLER , and _____, hereinafter referred to as BUYER.
This agreement is entered into between BUYER and SELLER for the trial period and purchase on the horse described below on the following terms and conditions:

Name:

Age:

Height:

Color:

Breed:

Sex:

Registration:

A. SALE PRICE
For the full purchase/sale price of $_____, SELLER agrees to sell BUYER the horse described in this agreement pending trial period as described below, and BUYER agrees to the terms set forth in this agreement.

B. PAYMENT TERMS
A 10% deposit in the amount of $ _____ is due prior to trial period. The balance of the down payment in the amount of $_____ shall be paid on or before _____, by cashier s check, hand delivered or sent via Federal Express to be received on or before _____. The balance of $ _____ shall be paid by postal money order or cashier s check in monthly payments of $_____ or more until the full purchase price of $_____ has been paid in full. Payments shall commence on _____, due on or before the first day of each month and a late fee of $20.00 shall be billed for any payment received after the fifth day of each month.

C. SECURITY
To secure the payments and duties of this obligation, SELLER retains a security interest in the horse. Should BUYER default in any terms of this Agreement, SELLER may foreclose on his security interest in any manner provided by law.

D. TRIAL PERIOD

BUYER has a trial period of _____ days commencing on _____, and ending _____. While under the trial period, BUYER agrees to the following conditions:

1) BUYER agrees to be financial responsible for transportation of the horse from SELLER s stable to and from BUYER s stable.

2) BUYER agrees to keep said horse in good health, and free from disease by providing adequate feed, shelter, and veterinary and blacksmith care in accordance with accepted industry standards.

3) BUYER agrees to keep said horse free from all liens and encumbrances and to pay any and all expenses levied against said horse when due.

4) BUYER is required to obtain and maintain mortality, major medical and loss-of-use insurance for the full purchase amount to be in effect before hauling the horse out for trial and kept in effect until horse is paid in full and full bill of sale is received.

5) BUYER is required to pay for the horse in the agreed upon manner or return the horse if the horse does not prove suitable for the intended purpose. BUYER agrees that if said horse should get injured or become lame during the trial period, it is the BUYER s responsibility to return the horse in the same condition as when delivered. Buyer is responsible for the full purchase price in the event of horse becoming lame, injured, or dead during the trial period or any time while payments are being made. BUYER is responsible for initiating and following up on all insurance claims. BUYER is responsible for making all payments on time regardless of when insurance claim payment is received.

E. VETERINARY PREPURCHASE EXAM

BUYER must order prepurchase veterinary exam to be conducted at BUYER s expense, during the trial period. Buyer agrees to either pay for the horse in the agreed upon manner or to return the horse if the vet exam is not satisfactory.

F. WARRANTIES

SELLER MAKES NO WARRANTIES EXPRESSED OR IMPLIED, INCLUDING THE WARRANTIES OF FITNESS FOR ANY PARTICULAR PURPOSE OTHER THAN HAVING CLEAR TITLE TO SAID HORSE. BUYER IS TO DETERMINE FITNESS FOR BUYER S REQUIREMENTS DURING THE TRIAL PERIOD AND SHALL DETERMINE PHYSICAL FITNESS BY VETERINARY PREPURCHASE EXAM.

G. OWNERSHIP TRANSFER

Upon payment in full, SELLER agrees to execute a BILL OF SALE to transfer ownership to BUYER, after all funds have cleared SELLER s bank. These documents shall be mailed via Certified Mail through US Postal Service to BUYER s residence upon verification of funds clearing SELLER s bank.

H. RISK OF LOSS

Effective the moment the horse leaves SELLER s barn, BUYER shall assume all expenses that are not covered by SELLER s Mortality, Major Medical and Loss Of Use Insurance, related to any accident, illness, or other peril that may occur including death or permanent disability of horse. This RISK OF LOSS continues until horse is returned to SELLER s stable or payment is made in full to purchase the horse.

I. LIABILITY

Effective the moment the horse leaves SELLER s stable, BUYER assumes full liability and agrees to indemnify and hold SELLER, SELLER s AGENT and any other parties related to this sale, harmless from any damage or injury to any animal, person or property caused to or by said horse including death to person, animal or destruction of property.

J. LAW

The terms of this Agreement and disputes developing thereunder shall be enforced and construed in accordance with the laws of the State of California.

K. DEFAULT

Upon default of payment by BUYER, SELLER shall repossess said horse and terminate this Agreement for Cause. BUYER shall FORFEIT any moneys paid prior to termination of this Agreement under default of payment. Default of payment is defined as any payment not paid within 15 days of due date. In addition, material breach of this Agreement shall terminate same. In the event of a breach, the other party shall have the right to recover from the breaching party all reasonable attorney s fees and court costs.

L. JURISDICTION

In the event of breach of contract, dispute shall be settled in Sacramento County.
EXECUTED THIS _____ DAY OF _____, at
_____, California

_____
SELLER s Signature

_____
BUYER s Signature

_____
SELLER s Address & Telephone

_____
BUYER s Address & Telephone

MENTAL TRAINING FOR HORSEMANSHIP

The mental side of horsemanship for humans is critical and something most clinicians and trainers spend too little time addressing. We spend so much time focusing on the horse, but until we understand how to truly communicate with the horse and ask them for behaviors, we cannot be completely successful.

Whereas the horse needs training, so do we. We need mental training. When talking about mental training, I believe we all need to understand that we must be very positive when thinking of our abilities. We must believe absolutely in what we are able to do. That means recognizing what our abilities actually are, no matter the level. We have to bring into account negativity. Why negativity? Because while we want to be positive about our own abilities, we also have to be realistic about where the horse is in his own training. Once we are aware of both the positives and the negatives in our relationship, we must not become overly attached to those ideas and allow them to interfere with our intentions; that is, the exercises we have planned.

Clear intentions are vital in training. We need to identify what our intended goals are. That includes where to start, how to get there, and where to end. We have to prepare to stay focused on these goals rather than to react to the environment around us. You may be working with your horse and have another horse get totally out of control or hear another rider shouting at someone, but you have to stay utterly focused on the horse you are working with. Find your center and stay on track with your own work. Don't allow yourself to get distracted, and you will find that your horse is much less likely to get distracted as well. If you are focused, your horse will be focused—it really is that straightforward.

Many people don't recognize what intentions really mean in terms of horsemanship, and yet that really is the magic in training. The Dictionary.com Web site's definition of the word *intention* is: "A course of action that one intends to follow. An aim that guides action; an objective." When we are clear as to what our intentions are, how we can achieve them becomes clear, too. The mental process actually provides physical form. As the horse reads body language, the positioning of your body makes the magical communication happen. For example, when you are out trail riding, if your intention is to turn right and go through a gate, you need to already see yourself doing it in your mind's eye before you begin physically doing it. The process may be difficult if the horse does not understanding or gets confused, but if you stay focused on going through the gate as you imagine it, this helps the horse. With any exercise we do, we have to be able to picture ourselves doing it every step. So imagine riding up to the gate, step, pivot, go through the gate, step, pivot to close the gate, move out away from the gate. If we cannot picture it, we will not be successful. If you can only see yourself going through the gate, then that's all you should do. Only do what you can actually perceive. Adjust your goals to meet your own ability to imagine.

Another important aspect is not to be affected by the horse's negative behavior. For example, if I have a rude, belligerent horse, I do not get caught up in his negative behavior. I remain focused only on the training goals. If we are working in the round pen and he bolts or charges, I focus only on getting the response I want, which is for the horse to relax; to have rhythm, balance, cadence; and to want to be with me. I am not worrying about the other behaviors—just focused on what I need to do to achieve my goals. That's often just a question of time, which is irrelevant to horses. They operate on their own time. But again, the mental image is key. You have to imagine the behavior and response you intend to get from the horse. It's the same with real estate. You can go out and look at a house as it is or see it as it's meant to be. Do you get caught up on a brown lawn and peeling paint, or can you imagine the house after you have worked on it and see how it could or should look? It's vital to learn to use your imagination to succeed. This tool is available to everyone; we just don't seem to use it often with our horses.

One of the reasons this happens is that we get so fixated on fear and intimidation. But in reality, those are normal feelings when being around horses! As a professional or even just a serious horse lover, you have to take that extra step, whether it's to go into a show arena or out on the trail. You have to simply get on the horse one day and allow the practice of handling horses to take on its own life. You have to be willing to take that chance, to accept the risk. And to do that, you have to be able to imagine yourself doing it with crystal clarity.

Many of the riders who return to horses as adults face this problem. They often want to give up or get overwhelmed quickly, which is no surprise. It seemed so easy to ride when they were young and falling off was not a big deal. Now that they are older and don't bounce as well, there is even more danger in handling and riding horses. So when you feel overwhelmed or feel like giving up, all you really need to do is back up in your relationship with the horse and return to the basics until you are more comfortable. Can that mean you may be doing just groundwork for six months? Maybe. So what? I have a client who was extremely fearful. She returned to riding in her late forties and got hurt trail riding shortly afterward. But rather than give up, she spent a year working her horse from the ground and then finally riding in the round pen, then the arena, and then at about the end of that year, went back out on the trail. She has been riding everywhere on the trail ever since. She did not give up. Instead, she reset her goals to be in line with what she could imagine herself doing. As her confidence built, she was able to imagine herself being more and more ambitious in her goals. Finally she broke through the fear barrier altogether and is now living her dream with her horse.

It's easy to lose confidence when we push ourselves beyond what we can imagine ourselves doing. So have confidence in your abilities, define your intentions based on those abilities, imagine yourself accomplishing your intentions, and then stay completely focused on working with those goals every time you are with your horse.

Focusing on your own mental state and preparation for your horse's training really is the most important thing that will determine your success or failure. What you can imagine yourself doing, you can achieve! So don't be afraid to dream big when it comes to your relationship with your horse. Believe in yourself; be patient, persistent, and consistent; and all of your equestrian dreams really can come true.

What do you dream about doing with your horse? The first step to making it happen is to mentally prepare yourself before you start training your horse. Picture yourself doing it and then next thing you know, you are on your way! Do you enjoy riding English?

A relaxing trail ride?

Riding bridleless?

Show jumping?

Or even just hanging out with a best friend who respects and loves you?

COMMON PROBLEMS AND HOW TO SOLVE THEM WITH ULTIMATE FOUNDATION TRAINING

For most of us, when we imagine our dream horse, the vision does not include images of bucks and bolts, a horse who won't load in a trailer, or a horse who displays any number of aggravating behaviors that make you want to rip out your hair and wish that you could ride a really big dog instead. How many of us have horses who are great on the ground, but have real issues under saddle? And certainly vice versa, a horse who is great under saddle but won't let you tie, bathe, or lead him easily! The reality is that once you thoroughly go through the exercises in this book in order and really take the time to get them right with your horse before moving onto the next level, then most, if not all, of your problems with your horse will disappear. Why? Because you will have learned how to communicate in his own language, you will have become his leader in your relationship. You will have learned how to ask for, expect, and reward the responses you are seeking from him. You will have established a solid foundation of training cues and responses that build on themselves to provide a stable, reliable riding partner, and by doing all this you will have earned his respect and affection.

However, in the case that you really do the work I have outlined and find that your horse continues to display a particular vice, this next section may be just what you need. We will review some of the most common behavioral issues that we see at my training ranch when people bring in problem horses. Now as I have been saying, the sets of exercises we have *already* covered are what I do with *every single horse* who comes to me for training, no matter what the goal is with the horse. When those are done consistently and comprehensively, they solve most of the problems we see.

However, once in a while we come across horses who may have particularly noteworthy issues, or more commonly we find that someone did not spend enough time on certain foundation exercises to really fill a gap that is creating the problem. I cannot emphasize strongly enough that you absolutely must go through the fundamental sets of training exercises before you move on these problem-solving techniques. There is a reason it's called foundation training! If you start to build a house before the foundation is set, there's nothing to hold the house up. That's just as true with horse training. You must do the core set of foundation exercises, beginning with the groundwork on through the saddle work, and you must be consistent and doing well in each step before you move on to the next level.

Once you and your horse have mastered these techniques, then you can look at how we work with the more serious vices that people commonly have to deal with. In this section, we will cover pullback problems, spooking, bolting, rearing, bucking, barn sour, buddy sour, cinchiness, and trailer loading. These are not all of the problems you might see, not by a long shot, but we have to save something for the next book.

Pullback Problem

Pulling back is an amazingly common issue. I talked about it briefly in chapter 3, but because it is such a common problem, let's address it in more detail now. I recently posted on a few horse Internet sites to get volunteers for pullback horses to use in a video I filmed in July 2004. Not only did I get dozens of candidates, but these were all horses who were local to my ranch! Seems like a ton of folks out there have horses with varying degrees of a pullback problem. The great news is that I have had 100 percent success using the method we will review now to fix this problem. It has worked without fail.

I call this exercise the Post Exercise, and as I have said, it both alerts me if a horse has the potential for pullback problems and it's also used to fix pullback issues we discover. There are two reasons why a horse has a pullback problem. Either he simply has not learned to give to pressure while on a lead line, or he has learned to yield, but in emotional situations the fear and flight instinct overrides the training to yield.

The reason for a chronic pullback problem is that the horse learned to pull back from feeling confined and somehow got relief in the past when this happened. The lead line or halter broke, and the horse got away as a result of pulling back. Once this happens, they will continue to pull back in the future looking for that relief again.

The trick is to train them to get the relief without giving them the release.

This exercise is also very useful for working with horses who are quite nervous around their legs or sides. It keeps us at a truly safe distance, better than a dressage stick, and is also good for farrier practice. Ultimately it teaches the horse to yield to pressure left to right and also to turn on the forehand.

To begin, I clip a tie ring onto one of the round pen panels. A hitching post or any sturdy rail will work as well. A tie ring is a training tool that allows the rope to drag through it without being tied hard and fast. When the horse gets excited and pulls back; they will feel a drag on the rope, which then releases their higher energy and nervousness. They get relief, but no instant release.

I use a twenty-five foot line. This means that if they pull back twelve feet, I have plenty of rope to go through the ring and still remain at a safe distance. And while I know it's still a common practice, I firmly believe you should never teach horses while they are tied to a snubbing post hard and fast. Horses who are very emotional will injure or even kill themselves trying to escape the pressure; without being able to get the relief they can really get hurt. This method allows limited pullback so the horse gets that relief, but *not* release. I have been 100 percent successful doing this with every single horse I have worked with.

Thread the line through the training tie and then attach it to the halter. Stand behind your horse out of harm's way. You will then start to slowly bump the horse along his side with the rope. If he gets nervous, keep bumping until he gets quiet; again, if for a split second, and then release. You need to be watching very carefully for that moment to release. Over time, you will increase the pressure, making the bumping and the contact of the rope a little more intense. If or when the horse pulls back, let the rope go, allowing it to slide through your fingers. The tie ring regulates its own drag to maintain some contact with the horse even as he finds relief. Over time, this teaches the horse to tie even with pressure or in fearful situations.

Once the horse is solid on one side, flip the rope over its back like a jump rope to the other side and repeat the steps. As the horse becomes more and more comfortable, you can add more excitement and energy to the rope. Anytime he gets in trouble, simply let go of the rope and let the tie ring do its thing.

You must address a chronic pullback problem if your horse has one. In the case of a horse I worked with last year, if you barely touched the lead line, the horse would rear up. He had actually flipped himself backward on occasion, driven by the intense emotional state and the drive for relief.

But even with an extreme problem like his, within two lessons of about thirty-five to forty minutes each, I could tie that horse anywhere. If done right, this really does work that well. In fact, I will initially encourage all the horses I have in training to pull back on purpose, just so I can teach them this lesson.

Now if you do not have a round pen, this can also be done at a hitching post or any other solid location where you can attach a tie ring.

At the beginning of the post exercise, this Arabian horse, Julian, is very nervous and pulling back somewhat. Because the rope is left with drag available, he can get some relief and does not panic.

Next, direct pressure via the rope is placed lightly against Julian's hip to ask him to step over and move off the contact.

Because Julian has not yet learned to yield, Charles uses more pressure to ask Julian to give in the direction of the pressure.

As soon as he starts to move off, Charles releases the pressure to reward the yield.

Charles swings the rope over his hip to work on the other side. He will spend much time patiently working him on both sides, progressively asking for more responsiveness as Julian learns to yield to pressure with less and less contact.

At the end of the exercise, Julian is totally relaxed, standing quietly near the railing even though he is not actually tied.

And Chantilly the yearling filly gets her first post exercise training in her own paddock.

Spooking

While we have talked a lot about emotional control, let me focus now on the act of spooking. What happens when the horse's fear level overcomes that control? How do you deal with a spooking horse on the ground and also while riding? What can and should you do when panic mode is setting in for your horse?

Among the most important things you can do as a horse owner and/or rider is to remember constantly that you are your horse's primary trainer. Remember everything that you do with your horse is training him. As your horse's trainer, it is critical that you spend a lot of time preparing him for anything you want to do together.

Spookiness is a tough issue, no question about it. Horses can and will spook in a variety of environments and you cannot introduce your horse ahead of time to every object or situation that may strike fear into his heart sometime in the future.

The good news is that you don't have to. What you must do instead is to work on a comprehensive program of the emotional control exercises we have covered that helps assure you will have the control you need over your horse when something unexpected (and unwanted) does occur.

So preparation is the most important thing. You can actually eliminate endless spooking possibilities by really grounding your horse in foundation training exercises that are focused on emotional control. What you must believe is that nothing is more important than doing all the preparatory work. Do not just head out on the trail or to a show until you really have achieved good emotional control. Unless you have emotional control, you will not have physical or mental control and that is a dangerous situation indeed.

That being said (and my lecture delivered), I do want to address specifically what to do immediately when your horse spooks, either on the ground or while under saddle.

Spooking on the Ground

You are leading your horse or doing something while he is in hand and suddenly he spooks. What do you do? Most folks' first inclination is to try to get the horse to calm down by standing still. They will try to hang on to the lead line right at the snap, try speaking in a soothing voice, and try approaching the horse to pet it—anything to try to calm him and get his feet to stop moving (or flying through the air if you have a real emotional horse). Instead, we need to work with the horse's natural instinct. In this situation we do not have emotional control of the horse; the work has not been done and the horse is already higher than a kite.

What you need to do instead is let the horse release that energy in a positive manner. The horse's flight instinct has kicked into full gear; let the horse use that energy to actually calm himself. What you want to do anytime your horse spooks on the ground is to immediately start doing change of direction exercises, which accomplishes a couple of desirable goals. First, it allows the horse to be moving his feet in line with his natural desire for movement when scared. It releases the energy. But it also uses that energy in a way that still allows you to maintain control of the horse. With good line work, you are controlling the space and direction of the movement, which is also giving you mental and physical control of the horse. By doing the change of direction work, the horse is able to get his mind back on you and release all the nervous energy in a very productive manner. Additionally, you are also doing this work in the vicinity of whatever it was that spooked your horse in the first place, so you are also accomplishing some additional desensitization work at the same time. Now, your horse also needs to know how to do basic change of direction line work for this to be an effective method of dealing with spooking. So if you have not already done so, here is the basic technique reviewed again for the change of direction exercise.

Your initial goals for this line work are pretty simple. You want your horse to move forward in the direction you ask, when you ask. You want him to stop his feet also when asked. As you progress, you want his eyes and overall focus to be on you.

1. Ask the horse to move out clockwise around you. Depending on the training and emotional level of the horse, you can use whatever pressure is required (a verbal cue, rope, or lunge whip). The trick is to use as little pressure as possible, but as much as you need to get his feet moving in the direction you ask. No matter what, stay with it and follow through until the feet are moving. The instant the feet are moving, release that pressure to reward him. Only reapply it if he stops again before you have asked for a whoa or halt.

2. Ask the horse to circle around you several times (anywhere from four to twelve rotations), and then ask for the stop. To teach a horse to stop his feet, you remove the slack from the line and maintain the pressure until he stops. When you are just beginning to teach this, you will have to do more than just take up the slack. You will likely need to start with twenty, thirty, or more pounds of pressure to get that horse to stop his feet. Just as when asking the horse to go forward, the key is to use only as much pressure as you need, and never more than that, along with the immediate release of the pressure as soon as they stop (give). Your eventual goal is to have the horse stop his feet as soon as you simply remove a bit of slack from the line—lighter and lighter. This takes time and lots of practice. We don't expect success up front and even this initial lesson could take up to three or four hours, depending on how non-responsive (dull) your horse is.

3. Once your horse stops his feet, pause for a moment. The pause is very important for several reasons. First, it is a reward in itself—a respite from pressure and, since horses are by nature lazy animals, no movement is a reward in itself (when they are not in flight mode). Second, it helps teach them to look to you for what to do next—not to anticipate. Third, you are training in another fundamental building block lesson: the "stand." Your horse needs to learn to stand well to be mounted, at the wash rack, for the farrier, to be groomed, for lots of everyday activities, and this is where it begins.

4. After a five-second pause or so, ask your horse to do it all over again. Go forward clockwise several circles, ask for the stop, pause (praise as needed), and do it all over again. Do not go on to something else or change direction until the horse is moving out and stopping his feet well, along with keeping his attention focused on you.

5. Once those are happening consistently and the emotional level has come down, then you can change direction and start all over again, but going counterclockwise this time.

    Once this exercise is well established so your horse truly understands the cues, this becomes the fundamental tool to calm him down and get his attention any time and any place you have that need. Whether for trailering, shows, or anything new or spooky, this is the reliable way to calm your horse and center his mind back on you.

Spooking Under Saddle

When your horse spooks under saddle, typically he will bolt, crow hop, or even buck. Safety must be your number one priority in this situation, and that means getting physical control right away. You only gain physical control over an emotionally high horse through a lot of preparation work. So make sure your horse understands the cues for a one-rein stop so thoroughly that he will obey the cue no matter what his fear level may be. An effective one-rein stop requires that a couple of key foundation training blocks be in place. First, your horse must give to the bit well. If your horse does not yield to the bit, does not really understand giving to that form of pressure, you will not be successful. Second, you must have taught your horse to disengage his hips; that is, he must understand how to move the hips over. The one-rein emergency halt is perhaps the single greatest technique to stop a horse who is bolting or bucking. It has saved many people from terrible accidents.

So, assuming your horse gives well to the bit, let's review how to teach him to move his hips over and how to do a one-rein stop. Ask your horse to go forward at the walk. Then, working with one rein (it makes no difference which side you start with), put your left leg on the horse where you want to teach him the cue will always be, and pick up one rein to ask for the give. Now instead of releasing (either the leg or the rein) when he starts to yield, continue picking up the rein, bringing the nose diagonally across his shoulder, maintaining the pressure until his hips began to move over or even if he leans his hips. Release the second he gives you even the tiniest yield of his hips. Then move him out forward once more and do it all over again. Repeat this exercise perhaps a dozen times before you start looking for a more notable movement of the hips before you release. As you continue with the repetitions, be expecting greater movement of the hips before releasing the pressure.

Your goal is that eventually you will not even have to make contact on the rein. When you pick up the rein, your horse will move his hips over. The leg on the correct area becomes a precue, so that in fact your horse will begin to respond to just the precue. The horse learns to anticipate what is next and responds accordingly to avoid the pressure. Conditioned response is a wonderful thing.

This technique becomes your lifeline when your horse is very excited or out of control. Picking up on two reins when a horse is out of control does not help. All you are doing is capturing the energy and actually fueling it. By picking up on one rein to have the horse move his hips over, you are actually depleting the energy and giving it someplace to go. It becomes a constructive exercise. To prepare for situations where you may lose control of your horse, I recommend practicing this at a walk, trot, and then finally at a canter in preparation for one day when it could give you the needed edge to be safe.

Spooking in place . . .

. . . can quickly lead to bolting if you do not take the time to train the horse to react differently.

Spooking is probably the most common problem people complain about and probably the most common problem horses have because of their natural and amazing flight instinct. Considering that same instinct has kept them largely thriving in the wild over the centuries, it's hard to consider it a problem in every respect. However, for safety's sake as riders, we definitely do not want them doing something unexpected. So while no horse is guaranteed to be spook-proof, you can and should do all that we have discussed to desensitize the horse to a wide range of environments and objects and be prepared to get back hold of him mentally, emotionally, and physically in case something very unexpected and unwanted occurs. Invest the time now to make the difference later.

Bolting

The topic of bolting has to follow the discussion on spooking simply because, again, it's the most common reaction to fear. It is all about the horse's natural instinct, that impressive survival mechanism of theirs. While all horses get fearful, not all horses bolt. Some may buck, some get aggressive, and some may bury their heads in the sand. Just like people, you get different responses. Bolting is a common reaction and it's important to know how to school a horse around this problem.

The way to fix a bolting issue is to condition the horse with a different response than he has naturally had in the past. We need to change his natural reaction. We begin this on the ground, making sure the horse yields well to halter pressure. We start on a twelve-foot line doing line work, moving to a twenty-five or thirty-foot line as we gain more control. These are the same line work exercises we covered earlier; the goal is to ensure that the horse understands giving to pressure. We want them stopping their feet when we ask with just the lightest pressure on the line.

Despooking work comes next. Your initial focus should be introducing objects that you know your horse is fearful of and then working your horse around them and crossing over or by the object while remaining relaxed.

Begin with less scary objects, such as a pole. With the horse on a lead line, work on getting the horse to cross over poles. Anytime he wants to bolt, stop him immediately and have him change direction. This thwarts the behavior and starts creating a modification in how the horse reacts. He learns that when he bolts, he has to stop his feet and then do a little work, which causes some mild discomfort for him. This provides a reason for him to change his behavior (the bolting). When forced to change direction, the horse starts thinking about his reaction.

Next move onto to having him cross over two poles, then three poles. If any bolting occurs, you will do the same thing. Each time, stop him and make him change direction. Add in or transition to crossing a tarp and eventually you should be able to lunge your horse over a tarp without any adverse reaction.

Move on to doing these same exercises in the saddle. Teach the horse to change direction in the saddle and the one-rein stop. By doing this all as prior work, you set yourself up for success. This thwarts the behavior by modifying how he reacts. He learns that when he bolts, he has to stop his feet and then do a little work. If any bolting occurs, you will do the same thing even under saddle. Each time stop them and make them change direction. Just like the groundwork, add in or transition to crossing a tarp and eventually you should be able to ride your horse over a tarp without any adverse reaction.

This does not mean that your horse will never bolt again. What is more likely is that your horse will just spook in place and not bolt, which gives *you* the cue to pick up a rein and move that hip over so you will not be at his mercy. Horses usually want to bolt after spooking in place, so by moving the hips over, it gets them thinking again. Depending on how consistent you are, how fearful your horse is, and how much you work at it, this can be taught in days or months.

Rearing

People say that rearing and bucking are the two of the scariest things. Let's start with rearing. Why do horses rear? One reason horses rear is that they do not have forwardness established (they are either lethargic, do not have a good work ethic, or have simply not learned the go-forward cue) and when we ask for the forwardness, they resist. Now, horses have those six directions they can go: forward, backward, left, right, down, and up. Up is an escape route and it can be a very intimidating one. Rearing can be scary, and if we do not react to the behavior correctly, then the horse learns that rearing can *always* be an effective escape door and will do it again and again. Why shouldn't they—it works, right?

A horse will also rear when he does not want to cross an object. Whether this is caused by fear or stubbornness does not matter. In trying to get the horse to cross an object, we close off the left and right doors, leaving backing up as the horse's only option. When a horse backs, most people react by trying to drive him forward (with spurs or a whip), which makes the horse likely to rear.

Another cause of rearing is a horse not wanting to go on a trail ride or leave an area because it may be barn or buddy sour. We are asking a horse to do something that puts a lot of pressure on him (that is, asking him to leave a comfort zone) and we can be too aggressive in how we ask. Because we get so demanding in asking the horse to leave, we end up closing all the doors except for up or down, so the horse goes up.

To solve the problem with rearing, we go back to working on the go-forward cue. We work in the round pen with go-forward again, then go-forward work on the line, then line work crossing obstacles; then we do it all again but under saddle. The goal is to firmly establish forwardness from the horse when you ask for it, so that he will not resist.

Please keep in mind the following very important point for saddle work. When a horse backs out of fear or resistance, never ask for him to go forward until he has stopped. Once he has stopped his feet, give the go-forward cue and ask for it with serious intent. But do not ask until those feet have stopped moving. If you add energy and pressure to the horse while he is backing himself, you are much more likely to drive him up into the air. Instead, just try to relax and wait for his feet to stop and then cue the heck out of him to go forward. You have to give the horse a way out.

If you're on the trail or in a place where waiting for the horse to stop backing up may be dangerous, use your reins and legs to guide the direction he is backing to make it safer for you. But again, let him move; just make sure it's in a direction that will not take you over a cliff. Yes, I recognize that's easier said than done when you are panicking at the edge of a precipice. So practice it. Make this an exercise you do with your horse in the safety of an arena or round pen—learn to drive your horse backward. Just another way small preparatory exercises can become real lifesavers later on.

Even top riders have to deal with a rearing mount at times, but by keeping the horse focused on the forward movement at the right time, the rearing can at least be minimized.

Unless you're the Lone Ranger, rearing is really only fun while watching horses at play.

Bucking

Ah, bucking. (Imagine me shaking my head back and forth as I say this.) Bucking is kind of the "bastard child" of horse training. Everyone knows it's there and practically no one wants to deal with it. There are huge variations in what people consider a bucking problem. A horse can buck one or twice as a show of token resistance when asked to work. A horse can buck in fear, anger, and often in play. There is no question that many horses enjoy bucking; it just feels good to them. Then there are the horses who buck repetitively and violently. They will do anything to get a saddle or rider off their backs.

But whatever the level, as with rearing, we need to examine why it happens. When I get a chronic bucking horse brought to the ranch, I go through a standard evaluation with him to first rule out common causes.

First off, I always consider the pain issue. Poor saddle fit is frequently a reason horses buck. I do not mean to keep lecturing about this, but so many people believe they know enough to think their saddle fits their horse and it really does not. Until you have a trained expert evaluate the fit, consider that your saddle may be causing some problems. When a horse has something on his back that is hurting him, he is going to try to buck it off. He's just seeking release from the pain.

So I start with saddle fit. If that looks good, we then move on to a physical exam. I have worked closely with some fantastic vets and chiropractors over the years to help come up with a way to assess the horse's back, joints, legs, and other key pressure zones for pain. If I see any indication of pain or discomfort, we then have the horse treated by an equine chiropractor and/or vet before proceeding.

On a related note, soundness issues are often discovered during these checkups as well. The horse has not appeared to be off to most eyes and has just been bucking, but then during physical testing an actual lameness problem is discovered—which is often the reason for the bucking. Again, the horse just wants to escape the pain.

The next step is to check the rest of the tack for proper fit. Once we are sure that the horse is pain free, then we begin to evaluate the triggers of the bucking.

Safety is first for my staff, clients, horses, and me. So I do not hop onto a known bucker to see "what's what" with him. In my opinion, that accomplishes nothing. There is no point in risking injury when I can try to trigger the behavior safely in a round pen or on the line. So that's what we do.

We start every bucking horse from day one in foundation training. I do not care if they have been broke for years; they get completely reschooled from the ground up. We work them solely on the ground for quite a while as if they have not been started. This is because there is some hole in their training, some gap, that has allowed their own reaction to certain situations (fear, anger, or something else) to respond with bucking. Bucking has become their release, their reaction to whatever the situations are. So we want to restart the training to make sure that for every situation we can control, their response has been modified to be the reaction that we teach them the cues for instead.

So those buckers go back to "horsy kindergarten." We take the training in baby-steps and watch carefully to see exactly when, what, and where the bucking is triggered. This can help us evaluate if it's a fear response, in which case we need to work more heavily with the emotional level and emotional control/despooking exercises; or if it is some form of resistance, in which case we will work carefully with the horse to apply pressure on him in such a way that bucking is actually more work and causes him more discomfort than not bucking. We will give him a reason he can understand to change the behavior.

I have heard people comment that they think it's silly that we sometimes wait months before riding broke horses with severe bucking problems.

In my opinion, the people who try to fix bucking horses by putting more and more pressure on them without giving them a way out or a reason not to buck are crazier. The old "spur 'em through the bucking" or "lunge 'em till they don't buck anymore" does nothing but tire out the horse while also raising his emotional level without any productive outlet for the energy. They give the horse no reason not to buck and don't provide reaction that they can use as a response instead.

Horses with serious bucking issues, especially ones with high emotional levels, need the time and patience that reschooling offers. You are not doing your horse or yourself a favor trying to find a quick fix for bucking. Instead, find someone who will take the time to start the horse over, watch to see when/why he bucks, and then set up those situations repeatedly during reschooling so that the horse can be taught to have a different response other than bucking. Chances are that if you take this approach, by the time riding work begins, the horse may no longer buck. Let me use Allison's horse Bandwidth as an example. We spent three months on groundwork exercises with that horse before I ever climbed up into the saddle. When I did, I approached him as if he had never been ridden. That first day in the saddle, I mounted, let him stand quietly, and then dismounted. That was it. The next day it was a little bit longer with some walking, and then we went on from there. But that horse never again bucked under saddle with a rider.

Allison had taken that big, gorgeous palomino to three trainers before me. One wound up in the hospital, another quit outright, and the third had recommended putting him down. At the age of four his papers showed six prior

It's easier and safer to work on the root cause of bucking and address it from the ground rather than under saddle.

Kind of like rearing, bucking is fun to watch when the horse is just playing.

owners when Allison registered him, making me think the bucking had probably caused him to be passed along from owner to owner. Each of the prior trainers had a similar approach to his rodeo-style, prolonged bucking: hop on him
with spurs or lunge him till he drops. With a horse like Bandwidth, who has a
high fear level, all they were doing by adding pressure was adding fuel to the
fire.

I am sure that because he was a nice-minded horse, someone rushed his initial training. They didn't deal with his emotional level and he learned along
the way that bucking was a great escape when he got scared. All I did was show
him that he did not need to escape. That with foundation training there is
always an open door for him to take, that he can understand what is being
asked of him, and that he can feel confident and safe. Once we had that, there
was no more bucking.

So whether your horse is bucking from fear, resistance, or some other reason, I cannot encourage you enough to consider finding a trainer willing and
able to take the right approach, which is to figure out what your horse needs to
modify the behavior—unlikely to be spurs and endless lunging. Bucking can be
very dangerous but you can also fix it. Really, don't give up.

Trailer Loading

Trailer loading issues are one of the biggest hyped problems in the horse industry. People have trouble all the time loading and even unloading their horse.
Trainers have written volumes on the subject; it comes up all the time as a huge
vice that requires a horse trainer to deal with, and yet it is one of the simplest
things you can fix yourself.

I suppose I could devote an entire book to the topic, and I confess I do
have a video on the topic. But the solution to trailer issues is so simple it's
embarrassing.

The cure is the go-forward cue. You need to teach your horse this cue and
he must know it and respond consistently *no matter what environment is*. Long
before you use it to ask him to go into a trailer, the cue needs to be strong
enough to have the horse cross a large variety of obstacles and in spooky/fear-
ful situations.

You must do the prework before actually starting the loading lesson to
make sure the horse is comfortable crossing objects.

Practice the go-forward cue over poles or tarps until your horse responds
calmly and correctly. You should be doing the standard change of direction line
work and incorporating the obstacles into the exercise. Your horse also needs
to have a good strong backup and stop cue before you begin the trailer work.
Again, go back to the basics.

Once you do the preparatory work, loading and unloading is a breeze.

When you are sure the horse is ready to go with those basics, then you are ready to start working with a trailer, but you start slowly.

The first step is to determine the horse's comfort zone, or where he really feels the pressure of the presence of the trailer. Watch his body language carefully and when you see he is starting to get nervous, that's the general area to stop and do some line work. Start doing the change of direction work at that spot, and if you can use obstacles too, even better. This exercise will lower the horse's emotional level, reinforce the go-forward cue, and get his attention and mind focused on you and what you are asking.

Then you move him closer to the trailer when you see him relax. After he's learned to be calm at this distance, you move him closer again. Eventually you can move up to be doing the work right behind the trailer with the door wide open. Some horses can walk right behind the trailer; others you have to start a hundred feet away. So, know your horse and what he is telling you about his comfort and work closer at his own pace. Do not rush it.

Once you have done the line work right behind the open trailer door, you can approach the trailer and ask the horse to go forward just one step, one foot into the trailer. Stop and back out. Do this many times until the horse will quietly put one foot in, relax, and back out relaxed. When you have reached this point, you can then ask for two feet in. Do the same thing, two feet in, stop, and back out. Do this for as many repetitions as necessary for the horse to be consistent and comfortable.

The next step is three feet in, stop, and back out. Again, do many repetitions until the horse is calm and consistent. When ready, try four feet in, stop, and back out. When the horse is calm and consistent, you can ask him to stand in the trailer for longer and longer periods before asking to back out.

Take your time; you may want to break up the training into two or more sessions depending on your time and the horse. It is better to go slowly and not push the horse so the horse knows the cue 100 percent. By the time you have gone through this process, he will have loaded and unloaded possibly two hundred to four hundred times. This may take two to four hours at a minimum. For the next four weeks, review every three to four days.

Some other tips to make it more successful: Have the trailer door (and the windows, if applicable) wide open to make the space look as open and inviting as possible. If it's a new trailer, brace yourself and do your horse a favor by tossing in some shavings with old manure or such. They will find the odor greatly reassuring. Horses do not like new-car smell. As for the timeless debates over straight load versus slant, ramp versus step-up—guess what? They *all* work if you take the time do the preparation with your horse.

Buddy Sour

When we discussed understanding the horse early in this book, one of the things we talked about was the fact that horses are herd animals. They base their social structure and personal dynamics on herd mentality. So while some horses want to be with other horses more than others, they all want to be with other horses. Then we come along, putting them in stalls, paddocks, pastures, and such, and when it's convenient for us, we want to take them away from their friends for a while and make them play with us instead. Next thing you know your horse may be whinnying, stamping, dancing, and rearing. He may display any number of behaviors that makes it clear he does not want to be away from his buddy.

But we are often short on time and more so on patience. We insist on pulling them away from their buddy anyway. This only creates much greater anxiety and then worse behavior. We create the circumstances for an even bigger wreck.

With these kinds of situations, the more you try to force the issue and have your horse "go no matter what," the worse the outcome is going to be.

Instead, try this approach. Find a baby-sitter horse and head out on a trail ride with that other horse. For the horse with the buddy sour issue, ride side by side with the baby-sitter and have the baby-sitter horse slowly start to get a bit ahead of you. If your horse wants to catch up, let him. Then once he is quiet again, let the other horse pull ahead again. The key to success is to work in very small increments. Start with five feet apart from the baby-sitter horse, then do thirty or forty repetitions where you let your horse catch up and relax.

When he is no longer eager to catch up when you are only five feet behind, then allow the distance to go to ten feet and do the same thing. Keep doing a lot of repetitions, adding five-foot increments in the distance as your horse gets more comfortable being left behind the other horse. Eventually, the anxiety will fade to the point where you can let the other horse get out of sight completely.

Never underestimate how attached equine buddies can get, even if they come from different *neigh*borhoods (or should we say brayborhoods?)!

This same principle applies to even leading your horse away from a stall or pasture buddy at the barn. Walk away five feet, turn around, and go back near his friend. Let him relax, then walk him away five feet, turn around, and go back. Do the thirty or forty reps and then work on increasing the distance in short increments. You are allowing the horse to learn that walking away does not mean he will not see his buddy again, and allowing him to slowly increase his comfort zone for being away from his buddy, This may sound monotonous, but it works if you are patient, consistent, and persistent.

Barn Sour

Dealing with a barn sour horse is in many ways similar to a buddy sour horse. It's very basic work and requires serious patience and perseverance. The trick is to work the horse in his comfort zone and increase that zone over time. With barn sour horses, I start out going only five to ten feet from the barn and do their foundation training work there. I will then add new exercises that I do around the barn. Then we go into the arena to do schooling work, so they start to associate the arena with work. After we do the schooling, we go out just a little bit, either in hand or under saddle depending on the degree of severity of your horse's issue, and then come right back. Don't go far—just enough to leave the arena or schooling area in a way where the horse is allowed simply to relax and go a bit without having to work. Thus he is getting rewarded for going away from the barn.

Then I come back to around the barn and do more schooling: training exercises like shoulder control, hips over, side passes, leg yields—work that demands a lot mentally. Then we relax and ride away from the barn. But as I said, we may start with ten feet or twenty-five feet, and gradually increase the increments of how far we are going away from the barn. It's vital that you don't push it. Allow his comfort to grow gradually and you will give him the confidence he needs to lose the barn sourness.

Cinchy

A lot of people tell me their horse is "cinchy" or has a cinchiness problem. This means that the horse reacts negatively when the saddle cinch strap is tightened before a ride. There are huge variations in how cinchy a horse may be. For many horses, you may notice the ears going back a bit; in others, they may lay the ears back plus stamp their feet or even reach out to bite or kick you. Extreme cases will have the horse exploding when you prepare to tighten up the cinch strap.

Clearly, this can be a very dangerous behavior and also it's just a pain, frankly. Who wants to argue with a horse every time you want to ride? There is nothing fun about having your horse try to move off when you are saddling him or kick or bite you when you tighten the strap. It's not an acceptable situation and it is one you can fix.

Before we discuss how to change the behavior, though, let's understand why horses so frequently react to cinching in the first place.

First, it often happens because a saddle does not fit the horse well. If you have poor saddle fit and then tighten the cinch, it's the act of tightening the cinch that actually causes the pain—pulling the gear's weight onto whichever areas are being pinched or prodded. So if the saddle itself is the problem, the horse has learned to associate the cinching with the pain. I cannot say enough about the importance of a good saddle fit! I see so many problems related to pain: horses trying to do just about anything to escape pain and most of those issues are from an owner not taking the time or finding an expert to help them make sure their saddle really fits. So if you have a horse who is cinchy and have not already ruled out poor saddle fit, please find someone who really knows how to assess your saddle for your horse's conformation.

A second primary cause of cinchiness is that the cinch strap fits over what is a highly sensitive and vulnerable area on the horse: the belly. It's just a physical reality to be aware of; that's a very tender zone and horses are naturally nervous about contact around their stomachs. The point here is that horses have a natural inclination toward being cinchy, so it's our job to help them feel comfortable and confident when cinched up for riding.

Ideally, rather than having to fix this as a problem behavior later on, we start our horses right to begin with. Even with young horses, the work can be done at any time to help desensitize them to a cinch strap. My general approach to starting horses with a saddle and cinch is to take it in three phases or increments of pressure. In the first phase, with the saddle on the back, I tighten the cinch strap with just the lightest of contact against the stomach. I will wait until the horse relaxes, even for a second, and once he does, I release that light pressure. I then repeat the exercise, keeping the contact of the cinch to the stomach very light, and releasing only when the horse is relaxed.

In the next phase, we take it up a notch and add more pressure, so the cinch is tighter with firm contact against the horse's belly. However, it is still not as tight as it would be if you were going to mount into the saddle. I then use the same technique of "tightening-relax-release" until the horse is complacent. I then walk the horse off while the cinch still has firm contact but is not yet truly tightened. I then recommend doing line work with the horse while

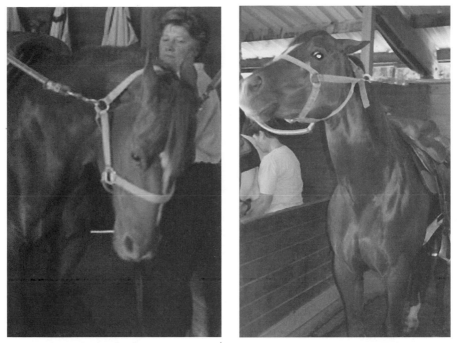

Lexi displays all the classic signs of cinchiness.

saddled to help him adjust the feel of the saddle and cinch. If he is a "puffer" (likes to put a lot of air in his belly during cinching), you may have to lightly tighten the cinch during the groundwork so the saddle does not slip. Again, you do not yet want it really tight, just stable.

After you have gone through the exercises consistently with your horse and he accepts the medium pressure of the cinch without reacting, you can then take it to the final stage and make the cinch as tight as it would need to be for you to be riding in the saddle. At the risk of sounding like a nag, (old cowboys never get tired of that joke, but our wives sure do), please make sure your saddle fits before you start really tightening the cinch strap of your saddle. Then, depending on what point your horse is at in his training, you would either continue to do groundwork exercises with the cinch very tight or else mount up for riding.

If you will be riding, a few minutes of line work before mounting can really lessen the chance of your horse reacting to pain or pressure once you swing into the saddle. To minimize the chances of your saddle slipping (which can really scare a horse and cause problems with saddling and cinching later) always double-check the tightness of the cinch right before you mount.

If your broke horse is already cinchy, we go into the mode of fixing an existing issue. The principles are the same but I will step back and start without the added pressure of the saddle.

I use a twelve-foot lead line, and then drop it over the withers, down one side of the horse and then bring it under the belly. You then twist the rope into a loop and slide the rope through to make it a cinch, in effect. Then do the same thing, starting with very light pressure (baby steps) and when he relaxes for even a second, release the pressure. Do it again and again.

As he gets more comfortable feeling the rope tighten and loosen, you can increase the rope's tightness, making the pressure maybe a pound or so of contact weight. Tighten—relax—release. Continue increasing the contact and pressure until you are at the level of tightness with the rope that you would be at with your cinch. Once you are there, you are ready to add the saddle into the equation. I put the saddle on, and then take it right off. On-off, on-off. It becomes a precue and you should keep at it until your horse gets used to it enough that he is nice and quiet when you put the saddle on his back. Once more, make sure it fits.

These exercises may take anywhere from three or four to five, or more sessions to get your horse past a notable cinchiness issue. If you are consistent and release the cinch pressure at the right times, it will go a lot quicker. But whatever it takes, keep at it. So many people just get used to having a cinchy horse, yet it's something that can and should be addressed, if only to rule out pain and fear.

Head Tossing and Pulling at the Bit

Some horses pull at the bit or toss their head around when bridled. With a lot of the common problems with horses, there is often a physical reason behind the behavior. So before we address changing the behavior through training, I believe firmly in ruling out any possible physical causes.

With head tossing and bit pulling, it is valuable to have an equine dentist check your horse's teeth. Sometimes your horse has the caps off his teeth or his wolf teeth will cause the head tossing or bit pulling. If the teeth check out fine, then it's a good idea to have the chiropractor come out for a visit. The vertebrae can sometimes be out of alignment, especially the first or second vertebrae, and when we make contact with the bit, it can really bother the horse.

If it appears there are no medical issues, then it becomes time to check the equipment you are using. First thing to consider is if you are using the wrong bit. Is it too severe? Is your horse ready for a higher level of bit (more leverage)? Bits should not be changed out lightly. There is an appropriate use *and* level of training for each type of bit. The more leverage on the bit, the more critical it becomes that your horse truly understands giving to the bit and that the rider has light hands, is riding with the proper amount of contact, and is releasing consistently at the right time.

Alternately, you may be using a bit that is appropriate but simply does not fit the horse correctly. Is the bit too loose or tight and resting improperly against the teeth? The correct fit for a bit is critical.

When in doubt, I always recommend going to a properly fitted snaffle. If you find the horse is still doing head tossing or bit pulling, then one of two things is happening. First, it may well be that the horse has not been properly trained to accept or give to the bit. If this is the case, then work more on training to yield and give easily to the bit. If your horse has gone through the right training to give to the bit, then it's clearly behavioral and almost certainly induced by humans. We are going to assume that is the case here and address the problem accordingly.

How many of you have witnessed wonderfully trained horses who were light and responsive become lesson horses for young or novice riders and seen them start to develop bad habits very quickly like head tossing, slow to go forward, or slow to stop? It's not the horse's fault, nor is it the newer rider's "fault." It simply comes down to that all-critical issue of timing and feel. Timing and feel take time to develop! It involves a lot of practice and doing it wrong at first. The subtle gives by a horse can be especially hard to recognize and reward. Also as newer (or unfocused) riders, we can often be concentrating on one part of our bodies while another part lets us down, so to speak. How many of us have in the past have kicked the horse while simultaneously pulling back on the reins? Or ridden with a lot of contact on the reins because we were nervous, without really ever letting up on it?

It's very easy to give horses mixed messages or simply to train them to perform the problem behavior because we released (rewarded) right at the moment they were doing the wrong behavior. It's not their fault. Horses seek relief from pressure. If we do not give them the release when they expect it, they will search for it. When riding, this often means throwing their head or pulling at the bit, as they pull trying to find release.

You can eventually ride with contact, but you have to teach them that over time; you don't start out this way. First, the horse has to really understand giving to the bit before you move onto the subtle nuances of riding with light contact. Even after you are riding with contact, when the horse gives, you have to soften every single time. There has to be a consistent reward when they are doing it right by giving them the release from the pressure they seek.

Fortunately, there is one very simple and very effective exercise to work on this problem with your horse. You can do this with either one or two reins (and you should be prepared to play with the length, contact, and anchor point a bit until you get the right feel). The next time your horse starts tossing his head, pick up on one rein, take out the slack, and fasten your hand to the saddle—I mean really anchor it there. With your hand anchored, the horse will keep bumping up against the contact as he throws his head around. When your horse finally quiets his head, even for a second, then immediately release. Once again anchor and repeat the exercise until the horse realizes it's far more comfortable to keep his head quiet than to be throwing it about. Do the exercise on one side for many repetitions until you can see that the horse is really getting it, and then switch hands and work the other side the next time the head tossing begins.

The real trick to making this exercise work is that we have to educate *our* hands, otherwise the problem will come back. It's all about timing and communication with the reins. You have to remain focused at all times on releasing/softening when his head is quiet.

Pulling on the bit and firmly anchoring our hand so it does not become a pulling contest is the same issue. Because if it does become a pulling contest, guess who will win? We let the horse do all the pulling and we simply hold hard to keep the position consistent. Then, anytime the horse softens or gives, we release immediately.

If this is a truly chronic problem for your horse, it may take dozens and dozens of repetitions over several days for your horse to really correct the behavior. But I assure everyone out there, this is a very fixable problem!

No Control: Stud Chains and Bigger Bits

Since we were just talking about bits, I want to focus this last discussion on problem solving of overall control of your horse and the frequent remedy many people seek: stud chains and bigger bits.

I am completely opposed to stud chains. Not only do I not use them myself, I do not allow their use at my facility. I know plenty of people use stud chains, but in my opinion, if we really love and care for our horses as much as we say or think we do, why would we ever want to inflict pain on them? Stud chains are used on the nose or below the chin, which are very sensitive, delicate areas.

I know that when a horse is out of control, we can get frustrated and can even get out of control ourselves. It's easy to take it out on the horse. But remember, it is never, ever the horse's fault. It is our responsibility to train the horse in a humane manner. You may argue that you have seen horses behave with a stud chain but the stud chain is only a *temporary* solution. Horses become desensitized to it, learning just to tolerate it. But take off that chain and that horse is again out of control.

It has been proven that in raising children as well as training animals, inflicting pain does not produce a learned behavior. The use of pain does not carry forward into the future positively. On the other hand, fear and pain can cause the reverse and create fear issues and negative behaviors that do carry over.

A learned behavior is when a correction is made and positive reinforcement is used that enables the brain to connect the action with the correct response. Then the behavior becomes a conditioned response and can be carried over into the future as what to do or what not to do. Although a stud chain gives *you* instant gratification, it is my experience that within a short while the horse gets used to it and all you get is a horse with a high head thrown into the air who is still pulling and dragging you off. Every horse I know of who is using a stud chain is still out of control.

Working with problem horses for the past twelve years has shown me that stud chains do not work. There is no positive learned behavior. The horse has to have a reason to make a change. If you do it through his mind with mental control, you have a learned behavior. Inflicting pain does not motivate horses to change. It only intimidates them and they become used to the pain.

Why inflict pain when we can train any horse, even a stallion, to respond to cues and behave like a gentleman? They are happier, calmer, and better partners. The difference is that the stud chain is a quick fix. Training is a time investment that will be worth it in the future, if you want have a responsive, light horse and to truly enjoy your horse.

The use of bigger bits for more control is very much a similar issue. We look to bigger or more severe bits to get the control we seek. Instead, the horse needs to learn to yield to the bit rather than you using a stronger bit. You want your horse to be light laterally and soft and supple. This is done by teaching the gives, not by using a harsh bit that creates pain for the animal, especially if he has not yet learned to give and the rider may be riding with far more contact (pressure) than is appropriate.

If you start by using a more severe bit, which puts more pressure on the animal's mouth, you will get likely control—for a period of time. What happens is that the pressure on the mouth and the severe bit will mean less and less to the horse. Eventually pressure and the most severe bit made will mean very little and you have an out-of-control horse. You also are not using the horse to his full potential; there is too much resistance. When being on the bit, the horse moves more on the forehand and does not fully engage the hindquarters, which means you are far from maximizing the horse's performance.

To start teaching your horse to yield, you need to learn to give/release when the horse softens and gives. So many of us create a heavy pulling horse by releasing when they pull the reins thorough our hands. We create stiffness and bracing by releasing when there is pressure. Since horses learn by pressure and release, when we teach them to soften and give to pressure, they become lighter and much more responsive to us.

Ideally, a horse becomes soft and willing to give, light on the forehand and able to use all the power in his hindquarters. Think of power steering versus no power steering in a car. If you can imagine the effort it takes to turn the front wheels without the power steering, compare that to a horse that is heavy and pulling.

Go back to basic gives if you need control of your horse. Start the gives by using one rein. Take up about four to six inches of rein to one side and hold until the horse responds by yielding and immediately release. You may hold for a long time, two minutes to twenty minutes if the horse is heavy and used to pressure for the first gives. Once you have asked for a give, you have to be committed to holding until the horse gives; otherwise, you have thrown away the cue. To stay consistent and maintain the pressure, anchor your hand to a spot on the saddle. You do not have to hang on; just use that spot to keep your hand steady. Once you have gotten the horse to respond to the pressure and you are getting a softening of the jaw and noticeable slacking of the rein, go to the other side and repeat. This is an exercise that can take hundreds if not thousands of repetitions. When your horse is soft and responsive on both sides independently, you are ready to go to two reins. You will be doing gives with both hands independently and you have to maintain the consistency you created by doing the one-rein gives.

Now you are ready to move on to teaching the same cues while controlling the emotional level. Do the one-rein gives first while adding distractions. Then practice at a faster pace or go over scary objects. When you have mastered this, you will have your power steering. You will not need a bigger bit to have the control you need.

The horse will always be vastly more powerful than we are, outweighing us many times over and always infinitely stronger. This means that they are able to break through any training equipment in a moment of serious panic. Harsher equipment not only causes pain, it can make your horse less able to control when you need it in those situations, not more. The only answer to gaining *and maintaining* the control you are seeking, whether from the ground or under saddle, is teaching the horse to yield to light pressure, no matter what its emotional level may be. It's no more complicated than that, though I recognize that certainly is a not an easy thing to accomplish.

But when you do, you are well on your way to having your dream horse!

IF ALL ELSE FAILS: FINDING THE RIGHT TRAINER

Should the time come that you've tried everything and are still facing some situation or behavior with your horse that you have been unable to positively change, it's okay to seek help. But it's just as important to find the right trainer to work with as it was for you to seek out the right horse.

We are very fortunate to have a lot of great horse trainers in this country. And yet tens of thousands of horses change hands each year because their owners find them unmanageable or undesirable. Passed from home to home, these unwanted horses often end up standing unused or worse. Bored and lonely, their issues may only intensify. Many of these horses are put into training, but often owners do not make the effort to find the right trainer. It is vital to find the right trainer for your horse's issue and more importantly, for you.

When looking for a trainer, consider these points:

1. Find a trainer who specializes in addressing your specific needs. If your horse has a severe behavioral issue, for example, even the best reining trainer in the world may not be the person to correct rearing. Find a trainer recommended specifically for your need.

2. The cost of the training should not be a primary deciding factor in whom you choose. If you add up the complete cost of owning a horse over even just several years, the most expensive trainer will be a small part of that overall cost. What is the value of having a horse who is truly

what you want in terms of attitude, performance, and behavior? While the old saying "you get what you pay for" can be true, there are certainly high-priced trainers whom I would never recommend and very low-priced trainers who are incredible. My point is to look not at the price of the training, only at the quality.

3. Seek out a trainer who will place just as much (if not more) emphasis on training you as your horse. It doesn't matter how good your horse behaves for that trainer; if you don't learn to get (and maintain) those same results, you've wasted your money. An integral part of the training program should be the extensive lessons you take. You must be schooled in the training cues alongside your horse.

4. Before you place your horse in training with anyone, not only should you seek out a lot of references from like-minded horse owners, but take plenty of time to observe their methods. Whether you audit a clinic or simply observe them training other individuals' horses, you should insist on viewing their work at length before placing a horse with them. You should feel both confident in their skills and comfortable with their style and methods before committing yourself and your horse to their care. Likewise, ask them for references from clients who have brought in horses for similar training needs.

5. Once you decide you want to work with a trainer, sit down for an honest and detailed conversation about your expectations and what they will deliver. I am suspect when people commit to specific timetables for working with horses. Until you have actually spent some time working the horse, getting a feel for its emotional, mental, and physical aspects, along with determining what the training gaps may be, it is very hard to promise a 60-, 90-, or 120-day fix. At best, ask for regular and honest evaluations, and be upfront with the trainer about what your back-out plan should be if things are not proceeding as you need or even as you can afford.

6. Once the horse actually enters the training, do not get complacent yourself. This is the time that you need to mentally commit yourself to be there 110 percent. Take every advantage to hone your own skills and work with the horse under the trainer's eye and guidance. After all, it is only about being able to duplicate the training on your own once you take the horse home.

Charles and Allison riding on a couple of their own dream horses.

If you have a horse with whom you are not happy because of behavior, ask yourself: is the horse not right for you or do you both need the right training? Most of the time, the answer is that the right training makes the right relationship. So if you truly value that relationship, spend some time and yes, money, finding the right training program for you both.

It makes all the difference in the world.

BUILDING YOUR DREAM HORSE

I hope it will not sound condescending if I tell you how pleased I am that you have read this book. Not because it's my book, but because you have invested the time and energy into learning more about horses and horsemanship and that's absolutely fantastic. Keep doing it! Read lots of trainers' books, go to a ton of clinics, watch videos. You can always learn something new. I know I do and every new bit of knowledge will help you be more successful in building your very own dream horse.

We called this book *Building Your Dream Horse* for a very specific reason. The Ultimate Foundation Training program outlined in this book sets the stage for you to do anything you want with your horse. It does not give you a finished horse. But it gives you a solid foundation upon which you can build the discipline (or structure) of your choice. It gives you a horse who is incredibly light, supple, responsive, respectful, and yes, I will say it, fun.

But the training only works if you work the training. And that comes back to those ten secrets I mentioned earlier: follow-through; control the horse's space; be consistent; have patience; be persistent; use pressure judiciously; release appropriately; it's never, ever the horse's fault; have a great work ethic; and most important of all, have fun!

I know the training program works because thousands of people—from true novices through experienced trainers—have used the techniques and gotten the results I have talked about. But they had to do the work, and in these days when we are all so busy with careers and family, finding that time to get the training work done right can be a huge challenge.

So when you are ready to start with your horse, set realistic goals for yourself and your equine partner. Make the time and training work for both of you. And no matter what, do not give up on yourself or on your dream. You can and will build your very own dream horse.

The Charles Wilhelm Training Facility

Success through Knowledge

This sixty-acre ranch in Castro Valley, California, is known for its picturesque setting as well as its friendliness and hospitality. The ranch is operated as a year-round training and educational forum for horse owners and enthusiasts of every level. At any given time you may find experienced trainers brushing up on their skills in the arena or on trail, while a novice learns the basics of round pen work. Ongoing activities include training programs, lessons, horsemanship programs, apprenticeships, clinics, and other educational events.

The center has forty stalls, a 100-foot by 250-foot covered arena, two outdoor arenas, two round pens, large outdoor turnouts, several outdoor paddocks, and a modern bunkhouse that can accommodate up to ten. The ranch has many beautiful trails, a stream running through the property, and a wonderful view of the San Francisco Bay area. Charles, his wife, Anne, son, Jeff, daughter-in-law, Severine, ranch manager, Karen Werth, and the rest of the staff work closely to make this training center the great success it is and to ensure that every visitor feels welcome and receives exceptional care.

TRAINING PROGRAMS

A limited number of horses are accepted into a rotation of full-time training slots that may last anywhere from thirty to sixty days or ninety days or longer. The staff specializes in colt-starting and working with what are commonly referred to as "problem" horses. The average training duration for starting or reschooling horses is typically four to six months. This, of course, depends largely on the training objectives as well as the horse itself. Since Charles and his crew are quick to point out that "it's never, ever the horse's fault," all horse training done at the facility comes with full lessons for the owner as well.

A horse is accepted for an open training slot after lengthy discussion between the ranch staff, Charles, and the horse's owner. All parties go through an evaluation of the horse's needs, as well as the owner's, to ensure that expectations have been clearly set and there are realistic objectives.

Charles believes that the extent of the horse's training is ultimately only as good as the owner/rider practice and what they are taught at Charles Wilhelm Training. Thus, the training of the horse is guaranteed to the last day of the horse's training. Once the horse leaves Charles Wilhelm Training Center, its continued success depends on the owner or rider. To that end and to fulfill each owner's training goals, owners are required to commit to a minimum of two monthly riding/handling lessons and are encouraged to take advantage of weekly lessons when possible. These may be scheduled as private, semiprivate, or group lessons, or may be supervised practice sessions. All horses in training or boarding must have safe ground manners that include respectful leading, tying, farrier, trailer loading, and stall manners. For horses entering the program, these are often early training objectives.

To protect each client's training investment, only Charles Wilhelm trainers and coaches will be allowed to school a horse (unless an exception is written into the training contract). And all clients are discouraged from experimenting with outside advice during the term of the training, as it may impede the progress of the client and the horse.

Charles meets personally at least once a month with every training client to review the horse's (and owner's) progress, and to provide a complete evaluation as well as discuss the next steps and goals.

C.W. Training believes that horses have an inherent desire to perform for their handlers but are usually confused by unclear signals or are locked into undesirable behaviors that were never corrected.

"In twenty years of horse training and competition, I have concluded that there are no problem horses—only uneducated horses (and handlers). All horses are trainable; all horses are salvageable. The most enjoyable horses are those with good manners that have been patiently built through a solid training foundation. Once the foundation is established, the horse becomes a quick, willing student who is eager to learn and please. In many ways horses are just like people, with different characteristics and personalities. Each one learns at a different level and length of time; some horses learn lessons more easily than others."

Problem Behaviors for Which Training Services Are Most-Frequently Requested

- Rears
- Bites
- Shies
- Kicks
- Paws
- Head shy
- Barn/buddy sour
- Nonresponsive horse
- Balks at creeks or bridges
- Pulls/breaks rope when tied
- Bucks

- Bolts
- Won't back up
- Jigs back to barn
- Bulges out on turns
- Falls in on turns
- Doesn't always stop
- Heavy mouthed/headed
- Does not come when called
- Incorrect lead changes
- No flying lead changes
- "My horse has a special problem . . . "

This last one is heard frequently! Call the ranch to talk with us about the unique problem that interferes with your being able to enjoy your equine partner to the fullest!

HORSEMANSHIP EDUCATION

Charles Wilhelm Training proudly offers one- to three-week learning experiences for first-time and returning owners. Our exceptional Ultimate Horsemanship Program provides a sound foundation for starting colts, reschooling, and remedying behavioral or gymnastic problems. This is truly an essential course for all horses and disciplines, and an excellent overview of our comprehensive Ultimate Apprenticeship Program. Participants are taught the full range of tools that Charles has developed to promote the best in the equine-human relationship, helping both horse and owner reach their full potential. Whether working with your own horse or with those already in training at our center, you will discover how horses learn each time they are ridden and worked with. For better or worse, even the most basic interaction with your horse can influence his behavior. Through the C.W. method, learn how to produce exacting responses from your horse 100 percent of the time, both here at the ranch and at home! With a maximum of two participants per session, this intimate and individualized program is personally directed by Charles Wilhelm and his expert staff. Onsite lodging is available for out-of-town guests. Consider joining Charles for the Ultimate Horsemanship Program: an investment for a lifetime of horsemanship success!

The Basic Skills You Will Learn

- Solving trail problems

- Round pen training for starting colts and for reschooling

- Go-forward cue and its many applications

- WESN lesson teaching the four directions on the ground

- Mounting—preparation and safe methods

- Giving to the bit—creating a light and responsive horse

- Bridging the gap between natural horsemanship and classical riding

- Trailer loading

- Controlling various parts of the horse

- Sacking out/despooking

- Building confidence in horse and rider

APPRENTICESHIP PROGRAM

Charles Wilhelm Training offers this exciting twelve-week certification program for owners. Based on the Ultimate Foundation Training method, it is designed to deliver the fundamental tools for success with any horse in any riding discipline. The program is divided into four units of three weeks each, given over any period of time. This format allows scheduling flexibility and time between units to practice and apply new skills. Each level is offered at various times throughout the year, though the levels must be completed in chronological order. Certificates are awarded after participants pass each segment.

Horses: Each participant may provide up to two horses for each segment. One broke and one green is acceptable. Stabling, feed, or use of our horses is provided at an additional fee.

Level One—Basic Ground School

- Training philosophy and principles

- Round pen reasoning—working with fear and attitude

- Leading—establishing respect

- Sacking out

- Correcting problem areas

- Giving to pressure

- Special topic: Assessing the condition of your horse and its readiness for training

Level Two—Ready to Ride

- Review

- WESN—four direction control in hand

- Mounting—go forward cue

- Giving to the bit—from the saddle

- Lateral and vertical flexion

- Trailer loading

- Correcting problem areas

- Special topic: Hoof health and proper shoeing

- Transitions—walk, trot, canter

- Ground control of hips and shoulders

Level Three—Gaits and Aids

- Review

- Side passing—control of shoulders and hind quarters

- Leg yields and diagonals

- College-level leading

- Teaching the lope or canter

- Transitions

- Collection and aids

Level Four—Trail Safe

- Review

- Starting on the trail

- Dealing with the sour horse

- Getting over or through obstacles

- Trail terrors

- Special topic: Chiropractic and massage therapies

CLINICS AND EVENTS

Our celebrated year-round clinics and special events offer something for every horse and every rider. Among these are the popular Ultimate Horse Camp for Women and Ultimate Five-Day Colt-Starting clinics.

Ultimate Horse Camp for Women

This unique week-long camp is for women who are either new to horses as an adult or are returning to them after years apart from these magnificent creatures. Ultimate Horse Camp provides women with the comprehensive foundation of knowledge and skills needed to create and maintain the relationship, performance, and attitude sought from an equine companion.

Limited to only eight participants per session, the lectures and demonstrations along with plenty of hands-on exercises expose participants to a tremendous education surrounding the art of riding, owning, and even loving the horse. Some of the many topics include:

- Veterinary Care

- Equine Nutrition

- Farrier Science and Soundness

- Understanding Conformation

- Buying Your Dream Horse

- Setting and Achieving Your Equestrian Goals

- Introduction to the Disciplines

- Dealing with Fear

- Grooming and Bodywork

- Tacking and Fitting Equipment

- Foundation Training Basics

- Groundwork

- Responsive Riding

- Despooking

- Problem Solving 101

- Safe Trailering and Loading

- Key Aspects of the Horse: Emotional, Physical, and Mental

A variety of experts will be on-site to host the lectures and clinics. Charles Wilhelm will be personally performing the hands-on work and instruction in the training and riding topics. Limited space is available for overnight lodging for attendees and their horses (if desired). Participants do not need a horse for this event. This is an educational forum for the novice. This event books quickly each year; early reservations are suggested.

Ultimate Colt-Starting Clinic

This unique venue is offered on an annual basis. Every year the Charles Wilhelm Training Center receives hundreds of inquiries from people all over the country asking how they should start their horse "the right way." These are horse owners who really want to do it themselves, or at least be highly involved in the process, but simply do not have the education and background to feel comfortable and safe doing the training work on their own.

This exciting clinic is designed specifically for those people who want to fully immerse themselves in a highly intensive workshop targeted strictly to starting a horse under saddle. Over the course of the five days, Charles will work with the participants and their horses to cover all the following topics and exercises in great depth:

- Comprehensive safety for both horse and owner

- How to make any horse a calm, relaxed, and willing student

- Round pen reasoning: teaching respect and directional control through inside and outside turns

- The go-forward cue

- Ground manners: lunging, line work, leading, and tying

- Sacking out

- Handling the feet and legs

- Introduction to the saddle and bridle

- Your horse's first, second, and third ride

- Directional control, backing up, and moving the hips over

- Preparation for clippers, shots, and vet and farrier work

- Building the right lifetime relationship with your horse

- Solving common problems: cinchy, cold-backed, bucking, rearing, bolting

- Creating a long-term, safe working environment for continued training after you both go home

There are plenty of opportunities to work hands-on with the horse, and there are always additional Charles Wilhelm Training staff available to ensure help is available quickly if needed. This clinic also fills quickly, as it is limited to only five participants; we suggest those interested reserve a spot promptly.

Dozens of Clinic and Demonstration Topics Are Available

There is a comprehensive list of the topics Charles commonly covers at clinics and expositions on our Web site. Any of these subjects can also be conducted at your facility or hosted at ours with a minimum number of participants. A current events calendar, which is updated frequently, can also be viewed online. Please keep in mind that Charles does travel nationwide and if you are interested in hosting a Charles Wilhelm clinic at your own facility, you can select from dozens of popular topics, or work with Charles to create a custom clinic perfect for your own needs. Visit us online at www.cwtraining.com.

Index

affection
    overdone, 74
    pressure needs, 74
age of horse, starting training, 123–126
anticipation of request, stopping, 62
attention, nose and, 62

baby give, giving to the bit and, 92
baby-sitter horses, buddy sour horses
   and, 159–160
backing up
    line work and, 70
    stopping and, 102–103
balance, line work, 62–63
barn sour horses, 161
behaviors. *See also* natural behaviors
    cues, 25
    motivation for change, 79
    negative behavior of horse, mental
      training and, 138
    pain *vs.* learned behaviors, 167
biases, physical aspect of horse and, 18
bit. *See* giving to the bit; snaffle bit
BLM (Bureau of Land Management)
  Mustangs, 123
body positioning of rider, emotional
  control and, 8
bolting, foundation training and, 150–151
bombproof horses, 24
bonding, respect and, 67
bucking
    pain and, 154
    pressure and, 80
    saddle fit and, 154

buddy sour horses, 159–161
bully horses, 21

change of direction
    crossing over object and, 87
    figure eights, 70
    line work, 61–66
    round pen, 49–60
cinchy horses, 161–164
circles, transitions and, 110
cold blooded horses, emotional aspect
  and, 12
collection, 114–116, 126
competition, emotional control
  and, 10
compliance, personality of horse
  and, 21
conditioned response
    foundation training and, 33
    introduction, 24
    natural behavior and, 24
    reward and, 25
conformation, physical aspect of horse
  and, 18–19
consistency, description, 29
control
    emotional, 7
    engagement, 107–109
    giving to the bit and, 92
    space, 28
counter-arc bends, 105
crossing over object, change direction
  and, 87